"Gary and I share a passion for servant leadership, although our stories are very different. My passion was with coffee, as Starbucks Coffee Company's President of North America for 21 years; Gary's passion is with health care at Palmetto Infusion. His book tells the inspirational story of how he discovered and realized the 'success paradox' in his business and life, in a way he didn't expect. I highly recommend this book to anyone, no matter what business sector you are in, if you want to become a better leader and create healthy success in your life through humility and service."

—HOWARD BEHAR

Author, speaker, adviser

"Having pushed hard to be successful as a player and coach, I could relate to success at all costs. But, as this book points out, what is success without a life full of love, family, and friends? For coaches of all kinds: read this book before your next team practice or client session."

—PAUL DOTY

Former lacrosse coach of the UNC Tar Heels

"For the past 30 years I've watched the mental health crisis ravage my loved ones, my employees, and my own well-being, all because of pursuing traditional success. I've had a long career as a leader in the creative industry and this is the first time somebody neatly upends everything you might consciously or unconsciously believe about success—that it requires hard work, that you can't have it all, that you've got to focus on profit at all costs, that your health and that of your employees are not important. This book is a literal life saver. It's full of inspiring stories and practical lessons, with a clear road map to breaking free and charting towards our own paradoxical success. This is a vital read for post-pandemic leaders."

—PAULINE PLOQUIN

President and partner, Struck Branding and Marketing Transformation through Creativity, mentor, speaker, board leadership

"As a doctor, author, documentary filmmaker, professional speaker, change and communication skills business consultant, I've repeatedly witnessed the toll that the drive for success takes on motivated people and businesses. The authors redefine success by rightly putting health first, for individuals and for organizations. That truly is paradoxical thinking, particularly because they can demonstrate how financially profitable this has been. For anyone wanting to achieve big things, this book will prove itself an invaluable difference maker."

—RICK KIRSCHNER, N.D., V.N.M.I.

Internationally best-selling co-author, Dealing with People You Can't Stand

"I can totally relate to the author. I've accomplished many of the goals I set for myself as a young man—scholarship sports, world travel, meaningful relationships, a life of creative endeavors, and financial success. But, to the degree that I was drawn into the world of business and finance without my youthful love and creative drive, I inevitably lost my grounding and peace of mind.

Those challenges made this book much more than an inspiring read for me, it's an experience—an interactive virtual workshop with exercises and online materials that guide me out of that lonely fearful world and back home. For anyone else suffering from too many hours in a loveless business state of mind, keep reading!!!"

—DAVID STANLEY

Owner Wheaton Creek Ranch, artist, designer, investor

"How different our world might be if *The Success Paradox* were required reading for every young man and woman as they set off to make their mark on the world. What if we dumped the paradigm of success as an achievement earned at the loss of happiness and health, to discover success as a personal expression of integrity that earned us both? After four decades as a 'successful' architect I am ready to go back to the drawing board for round two!"

—PAULA BAKER-LAPORTE, FAIA

Architect, educator, and author, Prescriptions for a Healthy House *(1st–4th editions)*

"I hit the wall early and rejected the traditional success story in my twenties, becoming a leader in several NGOs and progressive political campaigns. I totally relate to Cooper's amazing story and predict that this book will inspire many readers into a deep inquiry of what true success would be for them and will launch many 'turnarounds' into service-first enterprises of all kinds."

—GIGI COYLE

Co-author, The Way of Council, *mentor, consultant, community activist, trainer and guide in rites of passage and circle ways for forty years with individuals, NGOs, businesses and communities*

"Combining Gary Cooper's remarkable life story with a set of practical, hands-on, and at times counterintuitive tools and tips results in a wonderfully rich and valuable life/business framework that can benefit many. Independent of age, gender, education, profession, ethnicity, and religion/tradition, *The Success Paradox* shows how to create tangible abundance and purpose that come from releasing ourselves to a greater power for the highest service to all. This offering comes at a special time for our species to realize its potential to experience our collective consciousness by exploring that which unifies us as being far greater than what is perceived to separate us."

—NIRAJ MEHTA

Founder/CEO, Kilowatt Capital; cofounder, Coongie!

"I was the founder of what grew to be a large architectural firm responsible for innovative buildings scattered across the US (you may have seen some in Las Vegas). I know my dad (who had told me: 'If you're not working, you're a bum') was proud of my achievements. Success is rewarding, but it typically comes at a steep price. My loving wife convinced me to retire at 72. It took two years of therapy to be OK without a 12-hour workday. I wish Gary and Will had written this book sooner. But, it's not too late to benefit me, or you."

—BARRY THALDEN
Architect

"Knowing Gary for 15 years, I've witnessed firsthand his personal and business trials, tribulations, and successes. His positive transformation in all aspects of life has been phenomenal. I think his best traits are his disarming personality, being genuine, honest, transparent, and he's a wonderful listener. I learn something of value from him every time we get together. The business leadership ideas and tools Gary offers are invaluable and his book will help nurture a much-needed movement supporting mental wellness!"

—JOHN ADAMS
Retired chairman and CEO, AutoZone

"*The Success Paradox* blends a compelling memoir with a practical guidebook, taking us on a journey from the ashes of a devastated life through to the phoenix rising. A self-described workaholic, do-aholic, and alcoholic, Gary Cooper hit the wall hard. When given just one month to live, he let go to the fire of trauma and used it as a force for profound transformation. He shares his hard-earned footholds on the way to sustainable success.

While the arc of this hero's journey was literally deadly serious, Cooper and Wilkinson have crafted a book with humor, inspirational reflections, and practical exercises that show us what is possible when we come home to our true nature, surrender to something larger than ourselves, and walk through our dark night to become a light for others. This is a guidebook you will want to carry with you on the rugged road of life toward true success, sourced from the ground of being."

—SUZANNE ANDERSON

Founder, Mysterial Woman and author of You Make Your Path by Walking: A Transformational Guidebook Through Trauma and Loss, *and co-author of the triple award-winning* The Way of the Mysterial Woman: Upgrading How You Live, Love, and Lead

"*The Success Paradox* is not your typical 'how to succeed' or 'this is how I succeeded' book. Instead, it's a faith-filled story of a life full of lessons learned by someone who discovered that achieving success in the traditional manner was profoundly unfulfilling. He found another, much better way. Following from his remarkable journey, readers just might completely change their own personal definition of success in its truest form."

—JAMES H. MORGAN
Retired chairman/CEO, Krispy Kreme Doughnuts, Inc.

"I was engaged by Gary and his newly promoted CEO as their Executive and Business Coach at Palmetto Infusion, so I had a front-row seat for their transformational journey. Gary meets my criteria for a 21st-century leader because he walks his talk and is a lifelong student. Through this book, he is giving back by enabling us to learn from his remarkable experiences so we can focus on what really matters in our businesses, our relationships, and our lives. What a gift!"

—SHARON D. RANDACCIO
CEO, Performance Management Partners Inc.

THE SUCCESS PARADOX

GARY C. COOPER
with Will T. Wilkinson

THE SUCCESS PARADOX

How to **Surrender and Win**
in Business and Life

Forbes | Books

Published by Forbes Books, Charleston, South Carolina.
Member of Advantage Media.

Forbes Books is a registered trademark, and the Forbes Books colophon is a trademark of Forbes Media, LLC.

Printed in the United States of America.

10 9 8 7 6 5 4 3 2 1

ISBN: 979-8-88750-052-2 (Hardcover)
ISBN: 979-8-88750-053-9 (eBook)

LCCN: 2023903069

Cover design by Matthew Morse.
Interior design by Megan Elger.

Since 1917, Forbes has remained steadfast in its mission to serve as the defining voice of entrepreneurial capitalism. Forbes Books, launched in 2016 through a partnership with Advantage Media, furthers that aim by helping business and thought leaders bring their stories, passion, and knowledge to the forefront in custom books. Opinions expressed by Forbes Books authors are their own. To be considered for publication, please visit **books.Forbes.com**.

*This book is dedicated to my father, Charles S. Cooper,
who helped me develop the foundational values that I've built my life on.*

*I respectfully acknowledge the many men and women
who lost their way while pursuing their dreams.
This book is for you,
for everyone with a worthy dream.*

*This collection of true stories from my life with the lessons I've learned
are offered toward what my kids liked to call a do-over.*

Everyone deserves a do-over in life.

ACKNOWLEDGMENTS

Writing a book like this is an epic challenge. I'm grateful to my writing partner, Will T. Wilkinson, for partnering with me to pull this off. The team at Forbes Books here in Charleston has been way north of amazing. Kristen, Lindsey, Mindy, you've exemplified what we write about in the book: "relaxed productivity."

There would be no book without my family, who supported me through my extended dark night of the soul. For my wife, Kelly, and my children, Clemons, Gracyn, Marshall, and Sutton, thank God for you! I'm so sorry for what I put you through and so grateful for your forgiveness.

My two wonderful sisters, Gina and Christy; my brother, Chuck; my beautiful mother, Carol; my amazing father-in-law, Cotton, who's been like a second dad, and his wife, Charlotte; my brothers-in-law from both sides; my uncle Jackie and aunt Tracy and my cousins. My life wouldn't be complete without all my nieces and nephews! They really do make life worth living and make me want to be a better man every day. They saved my life, and I live to repay them, and I can say that without a shadow of doubt. Same thing for my two pastors, Don Williams and Tony Ashmore.

I'm starting to feel like I'm giving one of those really long acceptance speeches at the Oscars! I can hear the music .... But honestly, the support from my family, especially, has been just incredible.

There would probably be no company without our CEO, David Goodall. He's an inspiration to me every day, an example of someone who rises to challenges by reinventing himself way beyond his comfort zone. Sharon Randaccio, my coach ... what can I say about you? You saved my butt so many times (often by kicking it!). You're the best mentor a loose cannon like me could ever have. And my very dear friend Mark Tassi taught me a new way to live by only comparing myself to myself. This alone was life changing because I quit chasing people, prestige, and things to improve inside problems. Thank you, Mark!

And then there's my business partners, the staff at Palmetto, the doctors we work with, and all our patients. We're a team, a family, and we've become successful together on every level. My life wouldn't be complete without all my nieces and nephews! They really do make life worth living and make me want to be a better man every day. They saved my life, and I live to repay them, and I can say that without a shadow of doubt.

A big tribute to Harriet Tubman, a historical hero of mine. She freed herself and went back to free others. What an example of a meaningful life!

Most of all, I have to acknowledge my Creator. God saved my life. Literally. I simply wouldn't be alive had I not given my life over to a higher power. The physical, mental, and emotional healing that occurred, the astounding business turnaround ... I know who was responsible for all that and it wasn't me!

Thank you for choosing our book. I hope it helps you turn your life and business around. Miracles happened for me, and I'm sure not special.

There are plenty available for you too.

BEGIN learning and mastering the Success Paradox Lifestyle

Are you being your authentic self? Do you understand the value of helping others as a business priority? Are you experiencing financial abundance?

→ Access the Success Paradox Lifestyle Check In to establish your starting point on this learning adventure through the QR code below.

CIRCLE UP with the Success Paradox Lifestyle Study Guide

Download this companion to the book, complete with curriculum and facilitator guidance for creating small discussion groups in homes and churches.

→ Download the study guide through the QR code below.

LISTEN to audio programs for guidance through experiential exercises

Some of us learn better by listening than reading. Explore the inventory of studio-produced audio programs to accompany and enhance the written guidance in the book.

➜ Listen through the QR code below.

JOIN the Success Paradox community online.

Enjoy our online discussion forum. Connect with others who are learning and living the Lifestyle. Find out about coaching and training programs, live and recorded, online and in person.

➜ Register through the QR code below to receive regular updates.

Visit us online at www.successparadoxbook.com to access these free resources:

CONTENTS

PART ONE

PARADOX # 1: Surrender and Win

Three Principles

PARADOX # 2: Father Is Child to the Man

Being Authentic

PARADOX # 3: We Are the World

Doing Good

PARADOX # 4: Profit before Profit

Doing Well

PART TWO

PARADOX # 5: You Can't Get Here from There

Finding Your Why

PARADOX # 6: Why Is There Never Enough Time to Do Things Right,
But Always Enough Time to Do Them Over?

The Success Paradox Lifestyle

PART THREE

FOREWORD

IN THIS WONDERFULLY INNOVATIVE BOOK, you're invited to think completely differently about success and life. We are presented with thirteen eye-opening paradoxes that challenge us to reevaluate what success means to us and how we've been prioritizing what's most important to us.

For decades, I've been concerned about the dangerous imbalance in our working environments (and in our lives) between doing and being. How much of our soul do we routinely sacrifice in order to succeed at work?

As I read about the three principles in the Success Paradox Lifestyle (SPL)—be, do, share—I remembered a success seminar I gave years ago where I asked participants to make a list of their "Top 100 things to be, do, and have." There was a surprising absence of happiness showing up on anyone's list. I wondered: Isn't the ultimate reason we want success is that we hope it will make us happier?

For too long, too many of us have routinely forfeited our happiness and well-being in order to succeed at work. And it's not working.

Over the past twenty years, I've been researching and teaching about happiness. It's become undeniably evident that our traditional definitions of success are failing to make us happy. Though we have more than we've ever had, we're unhappier than ever.

If success as we usually measure it, fame, and money really were the keys to happiness, we'd have a lot more happy people in Hollywood and the C-suite (and a lot fewer in rehab).

Gary C. Cooper's personal story gives us a remarkable alternative. Here's a guy who was bankrupt, owed the IRS $500,000, had a company bleeding money, was in a failing marriage, was struggling with alcoholism, and was literally at the brink of death. Just six years later, he's sober, healthy, and happy; his marriage is revitalized; he enjoys an amazing relationship with his children; and his company is valued at over $400 million, with a compound annual growth rate of 35 percent plus.

In *The Success Paradox*, Gary takes us on his journey through a very dark night of the soul to a life that is illuminated and inspired. He offers us the transformational lessons he brought back that saved him and can help us avoid hitting rock bottom in pursuit of a success that doesn't deliver.

Through the riveting anecdotes and hard-won insights that populate this book, we discover a new path to success—worlds away from being a workaholic or a "do-aholic"—inspiring lessons and practical recommendations for enjoying a passionate, purposeful, and balanced life.

Each of the thirteen paradoxes described in these pages offers a revolutionary way to thrive in business. One of my favorites is the concept of "relaxed productivity" and the provocative proposition that rest and achievement can actually coexist.

As the introduction suggests, you can read from page one straight through to the last page or you can jump into any of the thirteen chapters and follow your own path through this hero's journey.

Whatever way you choose to read this book, you'll discover a new world where letting go to access and be guided by a higher power emerges as the most powerful strategy for creating and sustaining a successful career and a happy life.

May you walk away with a new definition for what success means to you and develop a wide-open pathway to create it.

—MARCI SHIMOFF

#1 *New York Times* best-selling author of *Happy for No Reason* and coauthor of six titles in the *Chicken Soup for the Soul* series

Success: the accomplishment of an aim or a purpose.

Paradox: a seemingly absurd or self-contradictory statement or proposition that when investigated or explained may prove to be well founded or true.

WELCOME TO THIS CONVERSATION. If we were at my family home on Pawleys Island, South Carolina, we'd probably be sitting together out in the garden sipping sweet tea, contemplating the marshes, and marveling at the Spanish moss hanging from the trees like runaway beards. And I'd be just as interested in your story as you may be in mine.

Instead, we've got these printed words, and it's a one-way conversation. But since this isn't a memoir, I won't recount my story in chronological order. I'd rather experiment with something more experiential for you, a sort of learn-as-we-go field trip into largely uncharted territory, exploring what I call the Success Paradox.

This makes what you're about to read something of a detective story, following my life and near-death journey over the past decade to reveal a radically different perspective, understanding, and formula for success.

What you'll find are stories, insights, lessons, principles, and practices you can apply to your whole life, not just your career. And they're often paradoxical, which means they may not make immediate sense. But that's not a problem, and here's why.

According to *Scientific American*, "After decades of research, there is compelling evidence that we are not as rational as we think we are and that, rather than irrationality being the exception, it is part of who we normally are." The article concludes this way: "Given what we currently know, our persistent belief that we are primarily rational could itself be an irrational belief."[1]

I love that. It's a sort of paradox in itself, right? And it might help explain why we keep chasing success the same way we have for the past two-hundred-plus years (obsessed with reaching number goals, competing like enemies, driven by fear, letting our personal success be defined by others, etc.). Chasing success is not working. In fact, it almost killed me. I was forced to learn how to think and behave differently.

> *We can't solve our problems with the same*
> *thinking we used to create them.*
>
> **—ALBERT EINSTEIN**

I chased the American dream like I was supposed to, and I actually caught it. Big money, lots of stuff, recognition … I was living the dream. But I was also a workaholic and an alcoholic, I was ruining

---

1   Elly Vintiadis, "The Irrationality Within Us," *Scientific American*, December 12, 2016, https://blogs.scientificamerican.com/mind-guest-blog/the-irrationality-within-us/.

my family relationships … oh, and a doctor told me I had one month to live.

Well, I didn't die, obviously! Instead, I recovered fully. I transformed my life and my company. It was an actual miracle, I believe. This wasn't something I read about; it happened to me, and I'm going to tell you exactly how it happened.

What I learned and experienced challenged pretty much everything I knew, especially the belief that success and happiness come from the outside. Like everyone, I actually wanted something else (but I didn't know it). I wanted to *feel* right. And I didn't. I know you know what I'm talking about. Nothing from the outside had been able to change that inside condition. Finally, faced with that terminal diagnosis, staring at the end of everything, I had no choice but to make an irrational decision:

> I had to begin doing the opposite of what I'd been doing before and what I thought I should do now.

WHEN WOULD NOW BE A GOOD TIME TO CHANGE?

Assuming ourselves to be rational beings, we've tricked ourselves into believing that we handle our lives in rational ways. I sure wasn't! I had the numbers, but my life was a mess, and so was my business, even though our bottom line said we were successful.

We're touching the tip of a giant collective iceberg here, and what's hidden under the surface is disturbing. According to a recent Gallup poll, only three out of ten employees are actually engaged at work anymore. That's crazy. Especially when someone figured out that a highly engaged workforce increases profitability by over 20 percent.[2] So how have things gotten this bad, and why don't we focus in to change this, like immediately? Because it's easier to keep doing what we've always done than to change, even when what we're doing isn't working. That was true for me, both in my business and in my personal life. Maybe you can relate. Here's a story that makes the point.

> *A young girl is helping her mother in the kitchen. "Mommy,"*
> *she asks, "why do you cut the ends off the ham?"*
>
> *Mother thinks for a moment. "I'm not sure. My mother always*
> *did it. Let's ask her." Grandma is puzzled. "I don't know. My*
> *mother always did it. Let's ask her."*
>
> *They give Great-Grandma a call. "Why did you always cut the*
> *ends off the ham before you cooked it?" the little girl asks.*
>
> *"Because the pan was too small."*

It makes no sense to mindlessly repeat a behavior that stopped being useful decades ago. But just like the grandmother and the mother, we often don't question what we're doing. The little girl in this story did, which gives us our first important clue: it's not about being smart; it's about being curious. So remember that as you discover paradoxes in the pages ahead. The new thinking Einstein is talking about is … new thinking!

It makes no sense to mindlessly repeat a behavior that stopped being useful decades ago.

---

2   Angela White, "8 Employee Engagement Statistics You Need to Know in 2021," HR Cloud, June 9, 2002, https://www.hrcloud.com/blog/8-employee-engagement-sta-tistics-you-need-to-know-in-2021#:~:text=Let's%20dive%20in.-,Only%2036%25%20of%20Employees%20Are%20Engaged%20in%20the%20Workplace!,spreading%20negativity%20to%20their%20colleagues.

The sign of true intelligence is being able to hold two opposing views at the same time and remain functional.

—D. H. LAWRENCE

It's time to change.

WHY THIS BOOK?

Jack Buffington was the son of one of my wife's best friends and a close friend of our children, growing up together and sharing an idyllic lifestyle here on Pawleys Island, South Carolina. Jack was raised in a loving family. He was handsome, athletic, and smart, and he had a great personality and a large group of friends. The girls loved him; the boys envied him; adults respected him and predicted a great future.

On August 28, 2018, Jack killed himself. His mother said it came totally out of the blue. "I think we all feel like if it could happen to our family, it could happen to anybody," she said. "I think that's one of the scariest things about this." Jack's friends said that he put a lot of pressure on himself to be successful. At the time, he was a junior at the College of Charleston.

"Suicide is the second-leading cause of death among people age 15 to 24 in the U.S. Nearly 20% of high school students report serious thoughts of suicide and 9% have made an attempt to take their lives, according to the National Alliance on Mental Illness."[3] But this problem actually transcends all age groups. The overall suicide rate went up by 30 percent in the ten years between 2010 and 2020.

---

3   "Suicide Statistics," Suicide Awareness Voices of Education, accessed October 10, 2022, https://save.org/about-suicide/suicide-statistics/#:~:text=Suicide%20is%20 the%203rd%20leading,every%20estimated%2025%20suicide%20attempts.

Jack's suicide broke my heart, and I felt called to help. Like so many, I had mental health issues. BTW, did you know that mental illness is more prevalent than cancer, diabetes, or heart disease? Probably not, because it's a taboo subject in our culture. I quietly suffered the desperation of living as an imposter, comparing myself to others and always coming up short, terrified that I wouldn't be able to pretend even one more day that everything was just fine.

Maybe I'm motivated because I wonder why I'm alive and a beautiful boy like Jack isn't. It makes me certain of one thing, that I'm duty bound to make the best use of this second act God has granted me—for me and my family, for Jack and his family, and for everyone challenged to make sense of this life and prevail through hardships.

My writing partner, Will, and I have formed a nonprofit, the OpenMind Fitness Foundation, to help move mental fitness into the mainstream.[4] There's no stigma around working out at the gym, yet addressing mental issues remains a taboo subject in our culture. We can change that. But I'm just a 50-year-old white dude who survived a journey through the valley of death. We need to hear other stories and we'll provide a forum for that on our website, to create a network that champions mental wellness self-care and community support.

FAITH

Like many Christians, I got burned by a church leader who was exposed for being less Christlike than he claimed to be. That turned me away from "religiosity" and toward connecting with my inner, spiritual nature. That brought me right back to Christianity, but now I pay attention to the message, rather than the messenger.

---

4   Learn more about the Mental Wellness Resources Foundation at www.mwrfoundation.org.

My writing partner, Will, had a similar experience, and we've met at the same place, deeply respectful for all faiths. We understand that what matters is the *experience* of faith, not just *beliefs* about it. We both had to face how messed up we were, sitting in those pews just like other "true believers." It took leaving and coming back to become genuinely faithful.

There's a disturbing trend of people leaving churches by the thousands and not coming back. In fact, according to a 2017 Lifeway Research survey, about two-thirds of young people (twenty-three to thirty years old) reported that they had stopped attending church regularly. Why? They said it was because church members seemed "divisive, judgmental or hypocritical."[5]

Jesus said, "Ye shall know them by their fruits." We have to walk our talk, and we all stumble. What matters is that we keep on going, that we know beyond any doubt that there *is* a loving God, and that we're grateful for this incredible gift of life. What we do with it every day proves the nature of our faith more than what we do on Sunday.

The title of the article where I found those statistics is "Christians, Let's Stop Fighting Each Other and Serve Our Neighbors in Need Instead." What a great idea! Remember, wolves isolate their prey. People of faith need to stick together and refuse to let beliefs separate us.

We do need communal worship, sacred music, and hearing the word of God spoken through other people. Being "divisive, judgmental, or hypocritical" doesn't belong in church and it has no place in our lives. We are here to serve and love our neighbors, not to judge

---

5   Chris Palusky, "Christians, Let's Stop Fighting Each Other and Serve Our Neighbors in Need Instead," *USA Today*, June 29, 2021, https://www.usatoday.com/story/opinion/voices/2021/06/29/american-christians-turning-people-off-church-bethany-christian-services/5370555001/.

or fight with them. After all, Christ's last instruction to his disciples, known as the New Commandment, was to love one another.

WHO ARE YOU?

My partners and I bought a company eleven years ago for $1.2 million, and now it's valued at over $400 million and growing at 35 percent annually. As success and profits soared, I discovered another paradox, well explained by online marketing guru Dan Kennedy:

> *There is a huge secret about income that only a small percentage of top earners in every field ever figure out and use to their advantage … The secret is that the higher up in income you go, in almost any category, the more you are paid for who you are, rather than for what you do.*
>
> **—DAN KENNEDY**[6]

A friend recently recited a list of impressive executive jobs she was hired for despite minimal relevant experience, all because her innate value as a person was seen and appreciated. Whoever hired her knew she'd quickly pick up the skills, and she always did. This suggests that specifics about who we are should be included, maybe even prioritized on CVs and job applications.

We won't get those big bucks Dan Kennedy wrote about, payment for who we are (not just what we can do), unless others value who we are. But if we don't know who we are, how could anyone else?

What shows up when you ask yourself, "Who am I?" Maybe, "I'm a father," or "I'm an attorney." But that's not who you are. Those are just roles that you play. You are the one playing those roles.

---

6   Adam Witty and Rusty Shelton, *Authority Marketing* (Charleston, SC: Forbes Books, 2019), 137.

So who *is* that one? Maybe you believe you're a winner, or a loser. Maybe you think of yourself as being creative, hardworking, lucky, someone who is consistently happy and grateful or sad … even desperate. This is super important because who we think we are determines who other people think we are. We can cover up our insecurities with fancy houses, shiny new cars, and big achievements, but if we don't feel OK about ourselves, we live under a perpetual shadow, the fear of being exposed.

Let's take a moment to play a little game:

Find a scrap of paper. Write down the date
and one or two words to describe yourself.

"I am … what?"

Stick the paper in your purse or your wallet and forget about it.
We'll get back to this later. Here's what I would have written,
back in the day:

"I am an imposter."

Turns out that I'm not the only one hiding behind success. Some of the most successful people, surrounded by loving friends, family, and even millions of adoring fans, just don't feel right inside themselves. Matthew Perry, the actor best known for *Friends*, just released his book, recounting how at age thirty—with fame and money (a cool million per episode)—he crash-landed in the ICU for a five-month stay and was given just a 2 percent chance of survival. He got addicted to Vicodin. He survived, but many others don't. Sometimes they are battling serious mental health issues that require treatment.

Bipolar depression really got my life off track, but today I'm proud to say I am living proof that someone can live, love, and be well with bipolar disorder when they get the education, support, and treatment they need.

—DEMI LOVATO

THE IMPOSTER SYNDROME

There's a real thing called "The Imposter Syndrome." Psychologists Pauline Rose Clance and her colleague Suzanne Imes identified it way back in 1978. When I read their definition, my hand shot up. "That was me!" See if this shoe fits you as well.

"Excessive perfectionism, self-doubt, a sense of low self-worth: this state of mind makes you think that whatever you do is inappropriate. You either feel like you're not enough, or that you're too much, you feel like you yourself are a made-up lie, and that sooner or later someone's going to find out, and your world will crash in shame and humiliation like a house of cards."[7]

That was me. I felt like I was on a hamster wheel, chasing what I wanted and running away from what I didn't want. It was more than workaholism. I was a do-aholic, trying to solve a "being" problem with "doing." This reminds me of a joke:

A man discovers his neighbor out on the street on his hands and knees at midnight. "What's going on?" he asks.

"I lost my car keys; they just dropped out of my pocket," his friend replies.

---

7   Intelligent Change, "What Is Impostor Syndrome & How to Overcome It," accessed October 1, 2022, https://www.intelligentchange.com/blogs/read/what-is-impostor-syndrome-how-to-overcome-it?utm_source=google&utm_medium=cpc&utm_campaign=16633212375&utm_content=&utm_term=&gadid=.

"OK, I'll help you find them. So you were somewhere over here?"

His neighbor pointed. "No, I lost them over there."

"Uh, I don't get it. Why are you looking here?"

"The light is better over here."

What did we lose? We lost touch with ourselves. I can tell you honestly that I had no idea who I really was or that it was even important to know! Of course, I didn't get that this was my real problem. So, I did what most of us do: I tried to fill an inner void from the outside by making money, buying things, and being successful in the usual ways. I just kept on cutting the ends off that ham!

As Johnny Lee's classic song says,
I was looking for love in all the wrong places.

I had confused my value as a person with my value as a doer. I wanted—no, I *needed*—pats on the head, those "Atta boy, good job, son" compliments, but as you'll soon learn, I lost all that (and almost everything else). I've since learned that everything we do gives us a perfect stage to perform on, but if we're not authentic, the "audience" senses something is off. And so do we.

> I had confused my value as a person with my value as a doer.

BEING AND DOING

This diagram shows the distinction between who we are and the roles we play. Those roles are not who we are, just like we are not the shoes we wear or the car we drive.

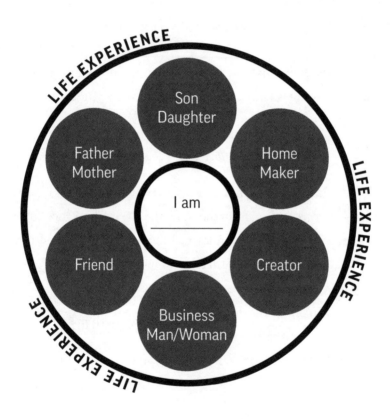

The second diagram illustrates what happens when we identify with a role. We can easily become obsessed and neglect playing other roles that are essential for a happy, balanced, healthy, and productive life.

This is exactly what I did.

This diagram shows what happens when we identify with who we are *being*, not with what we are *doing*. Just like that, we are free to change roles at will and enjoy the wholeness of our lives and relationships. Our fulfillment isn't dependent on any role; it's something we bring into every role, the value of who we truly are.

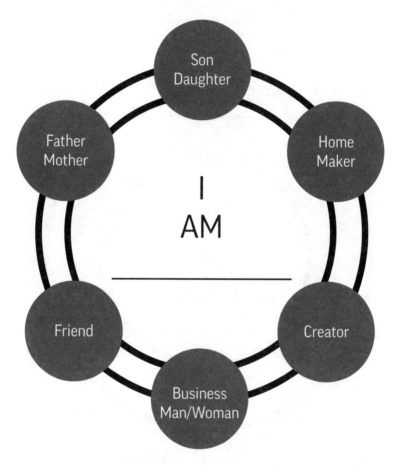

I described our book as something of a detective story. It's also a treasure hunt, and the prize is you! I agree with what a workshop leader once told his audience: "You're going to meet someone, someone very important: you."

THE ROAD AHEAD

We've organized this book into three parts, traveling through the three acts in the classic hero's journey. You can keep reading straight through, or you can jump around from chapter to chapter.

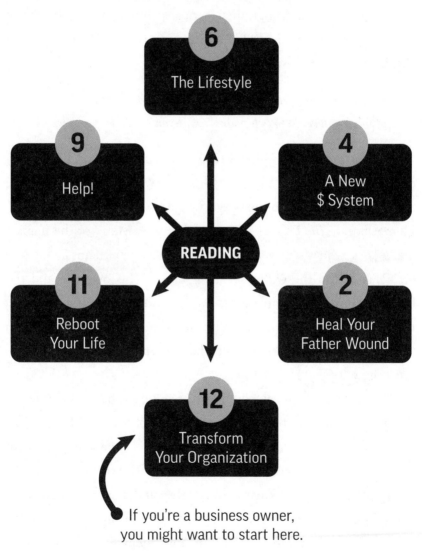

Read from the beginning
or pick a chapter, any chapter.

6

The Lifestyle

9

Help!

4

A New
$ System

READING

11

Reboot
Your Life

2

Heal Your
Father Wound

12

Transform
Your Organization

If you're a business owner,
you might want to start here.

You'll find worksheets and score sheets to fill out, audio programs to access from our website, and practices to experiment with, all offered to help you understand and experience what we call the Success Paradox. We also have a Glossary of Terms at the back of the book, describing what the various inventive terms we've used mean.

Heroes often traverse a magical portal into a different dimension. Think *Harry Potter*, *Avatar*, *The Chronicles of Narnia*. They find a secret door (or a wardrobe), they learn a spell to cast, and they often find an ally to guide them. Here's your door, your spell, your guiding ally, all in one paradoxical invitation:

> *Begin experimenting with doing the opposite*
> *of what you've done before and what you think you should do.*

Adventures often begin with a rallying call. Captain Kirk introduced every episode of the original *Star Trek* TV series with "Space, the final frontier. ... To boldly go where no man has gone before." Homer began *The Odyssey* this way: "Tell me, Muse, of the man of many ways, who was driven far journeys ... many the pains he suffered on his spirit on the wide sea, struggling for his own life and the homecoming of his companions." And Charles Dickens began *David Copperfield* with "Whether I shall turn out to be the hero of my own life, or whether that station will be held by anybody else, these pages must show."

You may be skeptical; you may fear you don't have what it takes, that your failures can't be turned around. Well, why not let go of all that? Let's take the symbolism of the Impossible Shape on our cover seriously and make the impossible possible. Dare to question everything you thought you knew about success and happiness. All you've got to lose is a shallow life, the constant fear of being found out, and a fake self. That's all I lost, and I don't miss them.

I'm not an expert. I'm a simple man who went through hell to get to where I am now. I just wake up every morning and do my best to live this new life. I still screw up, I forget the stuff you'll read about here, I fall, and I fail. But I learn from everything, I'm committed to be and do better every day, and I'll never quit.

Learning and applying the insights and practices Will and I have assembled here means that you never need to feel alone, or fear being exposed as an imposter, or compare yourself to anyone, ever again. What you'll discover in these pages can help you for the rest of your life. That's quite a promise. I hope you keep reading, apply what you learn, and prove me right. You'll need to leave your comfort zone, but it's better to do that early, before it becomes too uncomfortable!

BTW, you'll never graduate. All of us will be students of life until the end of our days. That used to bother me (I like achieving goals and moving on!), but now I appreciate the endless opportunities to learn and grow and help others live their best lives.

Our adventure has begun. Bon voyage.

NEXT:

Introducing the three core principles.

Coming out of your comfort zone is tough in the beginning, chaotic in the middle, and awesome in the end ... because in the end, it shows you a whole new world!!

– MANOJ ARORA

PART ONE

The unexamined life is not worth living.

—SOCRATES

The unlived life is not worth examining.

—WILL T. WILKINSON

Surrender and Win

Surrender is for losers, right?

Well …

*only if we surrender to another person
or give up on our dreams.*

But …

*if we surrender our will
to a higher power,*

*"Surrender and win" is the call sign
for true success.*

CHAPTER ONE

Three Principles

Vocation does not come from a voice out there calling me to be something I am not. It comes from a voice in here calling me to be the person I was born to be.

—THOMAS MERTON

BY ALL THE USUAL MEASUREMENTS, I was successful and living the American dream at full speed. I owned companies with revenues in the $30 to $50 million range before I turned thirty. I became highly skilled at buying, building, and selling businesses. I focused on helping people and creating social as well as financial profit. But my success came at a great cost to my health and relationships and accelerated toward one moment and one choice: change or die.

I've mused for years on how the miracle that saved me also inspired me to do a total 180, to defy decades of "proven" business practices and discover, develop, and finally write about what I've come to call the Success Paradox.

Surrender and win … that's a paradox. It's also my proven experience. But back in the day, I was fiercely competitive. If you'd floated this idea back then, I would have laughed out loud. Surrender? That's for losers! And I hated the idea of losing.

I was your typical hard-driving CEO. But living in South Carolina, I was also "charming." You may know the drill: sweet and friendly on the outside, chronically anxious on the inside. There are so many of us like that, driving to succeed the only way we know how. We're like ducks: everything looks calm above water while underneath we're paddling away like crazy.

I had a life-changing experience (literally) that turned me around. Now I don't just believe this paradox, I'm living it. What I call "relaxed productivity" turns out to be incredibly effective and enjoyable.

I've made more mistakes than most. I've failed at many things. I've hurt people. I've let them down. I've been blind, stubborn, arrogant, self-centered, and selfish. I almost died because of health issues I brought on myself through horrible habits, including alcoholism and workaholism.

Today I'm happy, successful, sober, healthy, and wealthy, blessed with a wonderful family, great friends, business partners who love working together, with staff and customers who feel more like family. How did I get from A to B? What can you learn from my journey to empower your own without falling as far as I did? That's what this book and the Success Paradox are about. If this sounds a little heavy, don't worry, y'all. I'm just a southern redneck at heart, and this story has a happy ending!

What you're reading is a product of letting go.

For starters, I had to let the dream of this book go. Two years passed before it came back. The old me would have worked harder and forced it to happen ASAP, I would have made mistakes, and the book would have been a failure. I probably would have hurt people along the way as well. Instead, I let it go. When the timing was right, the perfect publisher, Forbes Books, and my dream writing partner, Will T. Wilkinson, magically showed up.

> *When I let go of what I am,*
> *I become what I might be.*
> *When I let go of what I have,*
> *I receive what I need.*

—TAO TE CHING

I enjoy learning the history behind inspirational business books. In *Traction*, Gino Wickman writes: "This operating system didn't hit me like a lightning bolt; I've been refining it in the real world for over 20 years. It came through countless real-world hands-on experiences one lesson at a time."[8]

I've been experimenting for decades. I've joked that the secret of my success has been to do the exact opposite of what I used to do and what I thought I should do. But that's exactly what I did. My business strategies fly in the face of many recommended best business practices, but they work. The simple secret:

I don't make it happen; I let it happen.

This is also the secret to our bold invitation: surrender and win. Before we dive into the details, how about getting personally involved? It's easy to become a spectator as we read, but why not have an experience? Let's assume you're interested enough now to engage with this learning journey. You'll want to measure your progress. For that, you need a starting point.

Create yours by filling out this lifestyle check-in. This and all

---

8   Gino Wickman, *Traction* (Dallas, TX: BenBella Books, 2011), xv.

other Success Paradox forms are available on our website. You can register, download, and print out, or answer directly into the form below. If you register online, at www.successparadoxbook.com, you will receive automatic notifications every quarter, reminding you to take this questionnaire again to continue tracking your progress. Visit successparadoxbook.com for instant access.

The curious paradox is that when I accept myself
just as I am, then I can change.

—CARL ROGERS

THE LIFESTYLE CHECK-IN

For each statement below, check the appropriate box from 1 to 5: 1 for strongly no, 5 for absolutely yes, 2–4 for degrees in between. Trust your first intuitive answer.

	1	2	3	4	5
I am satisfied with my life.					
I'm ready to make the necessary changes in my life.					
I'm ready to make the necessary changes in my organization.					
Members of my family feel appreciated, valued, and loved.					
My organization has clear goals for success.					
I believe that self-discovery is an important determiner of business success.					
I feel grateful much of the time.					

	1	2	3	4	5
I feel sad at times but am OK with that.					
I am generous with my money.					
I believe everyone can be wealthy.					
I feel that being of service is more important than being successful.					
Our organization prioritizes customer service.					
I have a personal vision and goals for my life.					
My best friends know that I want them to tell me the truth about myself.					
I know my inner values and am guided by them.					
The true value of our society is measured by how we treat the least fortunate.					
I listen more than I talk.					
I am a good team player.					
I anticipate that this book could help me change my life and work in significant ways.					
I believe in a higher power (by whatever name) and feel personally connected.					

Total each column and add them together to determine your percentage score.

SCORING RESULTS (%)

0-24 Your honesty signifies that your current beliefs are significantly interfering with your happiness and success.

25-49 You are somewhat familiar with the underlying principles at play, but you aren't yet having the full experience.

50-74 You've begun your conscious journey to authenticity and are ready to test these protocols on real-life challenges.

75-100 Mastery is within reach. It's time to meet others like yourself and collaborate.

NOTE: If you register on our website, successparadoxbook.com, and fill out the form there, we will email you back a full report, based on which category you're in.

INTRODUCING THE THREE PRINCIPLES

What's most important to you?

When I ask audiences this question, I hear everything from caring for my family to following my passion, making a positive difference in the world, fulfilling my potential, helping those in need, being successful, etc.

What's most important to me now is being myself.

Conventional business practices prioritize doing, but I became radically more successful when I did the opposite. My focus on being may seem selfish, small, and narrow minded, but who we are being determines what we do. We create brands for our businesses and, increasingly, personal brands to establish us as an authority in our field. But what about our "signature," the unique qualities of who we are that are inside the brand? What about the authenticity that's sometimes missing in a media-manufactured authority figure?

A celebrity CEO who respects himself doesn't shame his employees, lie about manufacturing practices, or profit from products that harm the planet. A government official at peace with herself doesn't vote in laws that sabotage her constituents, just to pocket a bribe or get reelected. And when someone harms another person, it's a sure sign they aren't right within themselves. A teenager with healthy self-esteem doesn't fire an AK-47 at his classmates or commit suicide.

People who love and respect themselves will love and respect others. People who don't know who they are, who are conflicted, unhappy, and frustrated but place the blame outside themselves, may not even notice or care about the suffering of others, let alone be motivated to help them.

People who love themselves come across as very loving, generous, and kind; they express their self-confidence through humility, forgiveness, and inclusiveness.

—SANAYA ROMAN

I'm not a philosopher. Business has been my life. This is where I've succeeded and failed, celebrated my wins and grown from my losses, wrestled with my addictions, done my soul searching, and learned how to be more authentic. I've learned that:

People who love and respect themselves will love and respect others.

Every addiction is an attempt to fix something on the inside with something from the outside.

Changing things on the inside creates a ripple effect outside.

DOING GOOD

American architect Buckminster Fuller called that ripple effect precession. "One of Bucky's favorite stories regarding precession was the story of the honey-bee. Seemingly inadvertently, the honey-bee goes about his business of gathering honey. Precessionally, at ninety degrees to his body and his flight path, his legs gather pollen from one flower and 'accidentally' take this pollen to the next flower, resulting in cross pollination. The outcome of this seemingly inadvertent accidental activity is that the bee contributes enormously to life on earth. Of the 100 crop species that provide 90 per cent of the world's food, over 70 are pollinated by bees."[9]

Bees intend to make honey; we intend to make money. If bees inadvertently help produce most of our food (how cool is that?!), we can enrich the lives of all those we have daily interactions with. *If* we are authentic. That's some "side effect!"

I call this "doing good!"

No one is useless in this world who lightens the burdens of another.

—CHARLES DICKENS

---

9   Christine McDougall, "Precession and Integral Leadership," *Integral Leadership Review*, August, 2011, http://integralleadershipreview.com/3285-precession-and-integral-leadership-2/.

Compensation for CEOs is now 278 times greater than
for ordinary workers. That's a stratospherically larger
income gap than the 20-to-1 ratio in 1965.

—DAVID LAZARUS

Profits are essential to growth and to personal, corporate, and cultural health. But accumulation isn't the primary measurement of true success. Profits honorably generated by providing actual value can be shared equitably rather than hoarded.

I call this "doing well."

THE SUCCESS PARADOX LIFESTYLE

The Success Paradox Lifestyle (SPL) applies to the whole of our lives, not just business. It operates according to the three principles we just explored:

1. Being Authentic

2. Doing Good

3. Doing Well

I rank being authentic first because I know from experience that it *must* come first. "Success" was shallow for me until I began living as my authentic self. Shakespeare wrote, "To thine own self be true." Henry David Thoreau wrote, "Be yourself—not your idea of what you think somebody else's idea of yourself should be." Michael Jordan said, "Authenticity is about being true to who you are, even when everyone around you wants you to be someone else." Oscar Wilde said, "Be yourself, everyone else is taken."

When we know ourselves, we are naturally called to help others, and we *will* become financially successful. We may or may not live large lives, we may or may not create millions or billions in wealth, but we *will* contribute to the well-being of others, and we *will* have enough.

When our authenticity flows through everything we do,
we are helping others and generating abundance to share.

I simplified this even further:

The Success Paradox is about being successful,
not becoming successful.

I've succeeded in business and life by doing the opposite of what business schools teach: taking more time to rest, being a servant rather than a boss, listening rather than hogging the microphone, giving people options rather than ultimatums, etc. Everything I discovered and began practicing since my big turnaround has made me happier and made our companies more successful.

Success is not final; failure is not fatal: it is
the courage to continue that counts.

—WINSTON CHURCHILL

I was barely out of the woods when Jack suicided. That's when the "flash" came to me, the calling, an incessant inner voice that shouted: "You've got to help this next generation!" But I had to walk my talk first. I had to let go, keep on letting go, make being authentic my priority, and reach out to help others. When my own family really got that I'd changed for good, I felt ready to share what I've learned.

I realized that to help young people, I'd be wise to start with adults—so there can be people around to help the kids (leading by example)—and the best bet for that is movers and shakers in business. That may be you, maybe not. Regardless, when we help ourselves first, then we can help others.

We know the old value system that has contributed to this modern mental health crisis. "Efficiency management" has put profits first. It has squeezed maximum earnings out of our companies for over fifty years. Because so many employ comparison tools, they have also squeezed the life out of the humans working there. I'm not proposing that we do away with monthly P&L and quarterly earnings statements, bonus plans, and awards, etc. What I *am* recommending is adopting different priorities: be, do, share.

With the Success Paradox Lifestyle (SPL), you let go of the "make things happen" mindset. You focus on *letting* things happen by leading with your best self. This unleashes your God-given gifts. You only compete with yourself, not with others. Others become your allies … you genuinely want everyone to win together.

I was born this way!

—LADY GAGA

Socrates said that the unexamined life isn't worth living. My writing partner Will suggests that the unlived life isn't worth examining. Let's dare to look in the mirror *and* live full out.

A SIMPLE PRACTICE

We look in the mirror every day. We shave, we may put on makeup, we brush our teeth, we comb our hair. But do we ever really look deeply at ourselves? Used to be that I couldn't stand to look in the mirror, and I hated looking at pictures of myself.

This mirror practice is an opportunity to build self-esteem. If it feels embarrassing to do this, that suggests it might be a worthwhile experiment.

- Make full eye contact with yourself in the mirror and smile.

- Think for a moment about your life and those who've loved and helped you.

- Thank them silently. Feel the gratitude they deserve.

- They valued you, so value yourself by choosing a word or two and silently saying, "I am ..."

When you can look at yourself in the mirror and feel a spontaneous upwelling of self-love, you'll find it easy to feel the same way about others.

LESSONS LEARNED

- Paradox: a seemingly absurd or self-contradictory statement or proposition that when investigated or explained may prove to be well founded or true.
- This book is a product of letting go.
- What's most important to me is being myself.
- The Success Paradox Lifestyle (SPL) is described as "relaxed productivity."
- Every addiction is an attempt to fix something on the inside with something from the outside.
- If you want happiness for a lifetime, help others.
- Doing well follows from doing good. Doing good follows from being authentic.
- Being authentic flows through everything we do, helping others and generating abundance to share.
- Surrender and win.

NEXT:

The secret of letting go.

Father Is Child to the Man

"Child is father to the man,"
a William Wordsworth original,
means that the character we form as children
stays with us into our adult life.

"Father is child to the man"
means that fathers influence their children
to become adults like them
or in opposition to them.

It's necessary to disrupt that programming
to become our authentic adult selves.

CHAPTER TWO

Being Authentic

Authenticity is a collection of choices that we have to make every day. It's about the choice to show up and be real. The choice to be honest. The choice to let our true selves be seen.

—BRENÉ BROWN

I WAS TWENTY-EIGHT WHEN MY FATHER DIED of a heart attack. It chokes me up to write those words because it takes me right back to his wake.

It's one month before 9/11, a hell-hot day at the Mayer Funeral Home in Georgetown, South Carolina. Here I am, standing in numb shock as they file past; family and friends and business colleagues, senators, staff from the governor's office, and an endless line of strangers I'd never met. They are shaking my hand, muttering consoling words. I know they care. They loved my dad. Everyone did.

Sweat is pouring off me in buckets, but I leave my jacket on, I don't even loosen my tie, and I keep my eyes averted from the open casket. A few hours earlier, I'd pushed Dad's wedding ring back on his icy finger. Two days before, Uncle Donald had interrupted my golf game with a phone call: "Gary, your daddy's sick. You need to get out here." We raced out to our family farm and found him there, expired in the bathroom.

Today, I've got my game face on and my heart turned off.

I buried my grief with my father that day and began driving myself relentlessly. He'd had big plans for me, grooming me in business and even for politics. Now he'd left me to run a business with five hundred employees, $25 million in revenue, and ten partners older than me. Two months after the funeral, the bank called our loans in full. "Because of a significant change in management," they explained, and demanded that I raise $8.5 million.

The bank also called the $25 million loan my dad and his partners were carrying on their nursing home business, just to make it even more interesting for a young man who'd lost his father, the brains and energy behind the whole operation.

I scrambled like crazy.

I'll never forget the way partners, family, and friends all stepped up to help. Besides the tsunami of business crises, I also had to navigate a mountain of state and federal paperwork to settle his estate. So I did what my dad would have done: work, work, and more work.

That was his remedy for every problem, and it became my playbook. I managed to avoid bankruptcy and became successful, developing and selling businesses with revenues in the thirty- to fifty-million-dollar range. Some friends praised me and said Dad would be proud; others disagreed with my decisions and assured me Dad was rolling over in his grave.

I experienced exactly what the actor Matthew McConaughey described in his book *Greenlights* about his own father's death: "Even though my dad's no longer physically here, his spirit is still alive in me for as long as I keep it alive. I can still talk to him, do my best to live by what he taught me, and keep him alive forever."[11]

MY SHADOW LIFE

As much as I loved and now missed my father, I came to realize there was something wrong with the way he lived in me. I was suffocating under his shadow, haunted by the expectations I imagined he had for me, trying to prove myself to a ghost.

It's not flesh and blood but the heart which makes us fathers and sons.

—JONATHAN SCHILLER

I became a smart businessman, a good dad and husband, a contributor in our community. We raised our kids with three other couples, and I never missed a game, not even a practice. We had some great years. But I was revved up all the time, running my businesses like a reckless gambler, and it took its toll on my health. After more than ten years of out-of-control workaholism, keeping a lid on my feelings, fighting with depression, numerous surgeries, never asking for help, and drowning my stress in alcohol, everything fell apart.

Writing for *CareerCast*, Morley D. Glicken warned: "When work becomes all consuming and joyless—that is, you go well beyond what's necessary and have no other interests or activities—it becomes a negative addiction. Workaholics work because they have nothing

---

11   Matthew McConaughey, *Greenlights* (New York: Crown, 2020), 113.

else to take its place. Their work addiction is a recurring obsession, and typically joyless."[12]

Joyless it was. My only mentor was dead, and I was following him toward an early grave. I latched on to a couple of friends who were buying businesses to develop the largest homecare enterprise in the country. But now I had someone else to compare myself to, which made things worse. My self-destruction accelerated through an ugly three-year period that tore my health, my family, and my whole life apart. No one with any sense would have bet a nickel on my chances at that point.

I was hopelessly stuck in one gear and couldn't get out of it.

I wasn't just a workaholic; I was a "do-aholic." My addiction was to doing. I just had to be doing something all the time. And it didn't matter how much I was worth in dollars—at times I was worth a lot—because I *believed* I was worthless. I wasn't living my own life. None of my achievements felt like they were mine. I was stuck. I kept comparing myself to others and coming up short, trying to win, but every win was hollow … because I was a hollow man.

Success is as dangerous as failure.

Hope is as hollow as fear …

Whether you go up the ladder or down it,
your position is shaky.
When you stand with your two feet on the ground,
you will always keep your balance.

—LAOZI

---

12   Morley D. Glicken, "The TRUTH About Workaholics," CareerCast, accessed September 10, 2022, https://www.careercast.com/career-news/truth-about-workaholics.

Jordan Brown, blogging for the Mental Health Institute, wrote: "Feeling stuck starts with your thoughts. If you think you're stuck, you're stuck. It's as simple—and as complicated—as that. Thoughts create your situation. They frame how you see the world. They are, in fact, the foundation of your current paradigm. It's so easy to use your thoughts to create a convenient narrative about why you're worthless and can't go anywhere."[13]

> I wasn't just a workaholic; I was a "do-aholic."

That's the ceiling I was ramming my head up against, trying to reach and exceed my father's goals. But he was gone. His life was over. I was meant to live my life, not extend his, no matter how wonderful he'd been. And he was. My heart aches when I remember him. That line of friends at his funeral? There wasn't a single person there who didn't love and respect him.

A GENEROUS MAN

Buck, the family called him, but he was Charles Cooper in our community, where he was known as the Robin Hood of Health Care for South Carolina. Dad was the most generous man, a loving dad who inspires me to this day with how he treated me and our family and his friends.

It's Christmas Eve. Like every year throughout my childhood, we kids have piled into the back seat of our family sedan to drive around the neighborhood with Dad. We take turns running to

---

13   Jordan Brown, "Surprisingly Relatable Reasons Why You're Feeling Stuck in Life [With Solutions]," Mental Health Update, January 6, 2020, https://www.thementalhealthupdate.com/posts/feeling-stuck-in-life.

mailboxes with unmarked envelopes. Years later, I find out there was a thousand dollars in each envelope, given anonymously to friends in need.

Dad had always invested in the well-being of our community, even early on when he didn't have much. For many years he paid 100 percent of the health care for his employees. I remember the day when he wept because growth finally made that financially unworkable.

Dad was the most generous man I ever knew. But he was also a workaholic. Well, monkey see, monkey do. I became a workaholic too. He didn't take care of his body; neither did I. He had back surgeries, I ran forty miles a week to stay fit … and ended up having my own back surgeries. One day, it all caught up with me.

BAD NEWS

"Gary, I'm so sorry to tell you this, but you've probably got less than a month to live."

That's what my doctor told me. It wasn't a surprising verdict for a workaholic, a do-aholic, an alcoholic, an impulsive entrepreneur who ignored risk and lived with constant anxiety and stress. I was having regular panic attacks because I'd run up three million dollars in debt and owed the IRS another half million, even though I'd made a small fortune building and selling small companies. My wife and kids had lost patience with me, and my business partners were seriously concerned about business repercussions from my personal challenges, which was totally justified.

I wasn't putting a gun to my head, a rope around my neck,
or swallowing a bottle of pills, but I was killing myself.
I was just forty-five years old.

Meanwhile, underneath it all, every minute of every day, my father's ghost kept nipping at my heels.

As this comment from a blog on Psychology Today says,

Ideally, your father fills emotional needs to help you become anchored in life. It is a role embedded in how you learn and grow, and live to a ripe, old age.

Very few of us get to experience the idyllic picture of that father. When this happens, you meet a deep *grief* and a yearning for the "wished" for father. Grief can run deep as we watch others, creating a narrative in the mind of the self, whether true or not, depicting a better and more loving relationship with their father than the one you had with yours.[14]

Every father should remember that one day his son
will follow his example instead of his advice.

—CHARLES F. KETTERING

Maybe you've noticed how many films tell a troubled father/child story. Most of the Marvel superheroes have Bad Dads. Batman's dad was murdered. *Star Wars* has Luke Skywalker and Darth Vader (German for "dark father"). TV series like *Game of Thrones*, *Grey's Anatomy*, *Lost*, *Mad Men*, and even some of the old episodes of *Friends*, and movies like *The Royal Tenenbaums*, *Magnolia*, and *House of Gucci* all have main characters struggling to resolve their father relationship.

They rarely do. Heroes and villains duke it out with their bare knuckles, and the hero wins, or lovers embrace as music swells, credits

---

14 Edy Nathan, "Coping with Grief on Father's Day," Psychology Today, June 16, 2021, https://www.psychologytoday.com/us/blog/tales-grief/202106/coping-grief-fathers-day.

roll, and all those ghost fathers recede into the background, deactivated for the moment but ever ready for the next haunting.

And what about celebrities with father issues? We could fill a few pages with names: Adele, Drake, Miley Cyrus, Jay-Z, Beyoncé, just to name a handful. Bruce Springsteen offered some good advice in his autobiography, *Born to Run*: "We honor our parents by carrying their best forward and laying the rest down, by fighting and taming the demons that laid them low and now reside in us."

WITH A LITTLE HELP FROM MY FRIENDS

In the end, I didn't need a superhero to save me. My friend Mark showed up with some tough love. "Sure," he said, "you've got a drinking problem, and your body's a mess. But those aren't the real issues, and neither is your overwork, not any of the stupid things you're doing. Your real problem is that you're comparing yourself to others, especially your father. Stop doing that, man. Compare you to you! Just try to be a better you every day."

Mark cracked me open. Another friend finished the job. Big E, we called him, a gentle giant with a gravelly voice like James Earl Jones. He saw right through me, especially my fake faith.

"Boy," he told me, "I don't care if you believe in God as long as you don't believe you is God."

Big E helped me confront my arrogance. Sure, I went to church regularly and thought that I believed in God, but the way I was living proved I was trying to *be* God!

Lindsay Broder, writing for www.entrepreneur.com, described how she resolved her struggles after her father died.

In the end, I decided to let go. For the first time in my life I felt that the only thing I could do was consider the possibility that there really is something bigger than me or anyone on earth watching over us all, and guiding us through this uncertain journey we call life. At that point, I could actually feel it. I had been raised to "believe" in G-d but never really understood in my soul what that meant. At the time actually, I was calling it a higher power or "the universe."

I decided to let my higher power use me as a vehicle for delivering what I was put on this earth to contribute through my business and then something amazing happened.[15]

Let go of certainty. The opposite isn't uncertainty.
It's openness, curiosity, and a willingness to embrace paradox.

—TONY SCHWARTZ

I did what Lindsay did. Instead of trying to resolve the relationship with my father—even superheroes can't seem to do that—I let go. And I felt "it." The concept of a higher power became an experience. Immediately, my dad moved to a different position in my life, where he wasn't my primary model, and where his shadow wasn't looming over me. Now I didn't have to prove myself to him. And he didn't have to be perfect because something else was.

This forced me to confront something I'd missed, even as a regular churchgoer. I'd been treating God like a relief pitcher to call in for an emergency in the ninth inning! Now I realized that I had to *live* in this connection, not just panic connect when times got tough.

---

15   Lindsay Broder, "How Letting Go and Connecting with Faith Saved My Business," Entrepreneur, July 25, 2014, https://www.entrepreneur.com/article/235965.

THE CASE FOR GOD

Something is in control, and it's not me.

Something—whatever we call it—is running the universe. *It* is also managing to keep us alive. I learned that our bodies are made up of about one hundred trillion cells. Some intelligence must be guiding their growth, all from the division of just one original cell, right? And every sixty seconds about three hundred million of those cells die while the same number are created to replace them. That's incredible.

What about our brains? Apparently, the human brain is 80 percent water, holds five times as much information as the *Encyclopedia Britannica*, and draws the same power as a ten-watt light bulb, while nerve impulses speed around at two hundred miles per hour.

Then there are our hearts. They never rest. They beat an average of eighty times per minute, one hundred thousand times a day, thirty-five million times a year, and 2.5 billion times during the average lifetime. We have sixty thousand miles of veins and capillaries circulating six quarts of blood three times every minute. There's no battery for the heart, no wires … so, what keeps it beating? Whatever is doing that must have intelligence, right?[16]

The sun is ninety-one million miles away. Beneath our feet, each tablespoon of soil is teeming with over fifty billion living organisms, including one billion bacteria. Right now, this earth is rotating at one thousand miles per hour while orbiting the sun at sixty-seven thousand miles per hour inside our solar system, which is traveling 448,000 miles per hour to traverse the Milky Way in 230 million light years. Meanwhile, the Milky Way galaxy is spinning 130 miles per

---

16   "10 Miraculous Things about Your Body," All Pro Dad, accessed September 7, 2022, https://www.allprodad.com/10-miraculous-things-about-your-body/.

second (not per hour), while hurtling through space at 1.3 million miles per hour.[17]

That's astounding. We generally don't think about any of this, and we sure don't consciously manage it, but we couldn't live without *something* taking care of it all for us.

What *is* that something?

Those who leave everything in God's hand
will eventually see God's hand in everything.

—ANONYMOUS

Some call it God. That's a troublesome word for many people. Lindsay spelled it G-d, probably for that reason. Others prefer words like Life Force or Universal Intelligence. By whatever name, *something* is in control, and it's not you or me. Imagine trying to control everything I just mentioned. How long would your heart keep beating, how long before the planets crashed into each other, if you had to make all those decisions and calculations yourself?

This means that we've already surrendered control, unconsciously. Otherwise, we'd be trying to beat our hearts and plotting planetary orbits. We don't do that. So our challenge is letting go of what we *are* managing, letting go of inappropriate control, so that same organizing intelligence can run our tiny sliver of this Big Show.

Surrendering control to a higher power was the first step I took in turning my life around. Next, I had to learn how to let that power manage the details of my life. This meant firing myself as the CEO of my own company and delegating management and even decision-

---

17   Daisy Dobrijevic, Tereza Pultarova, "Milky Way Galaxy: Everything You Need to Know about Our Cosmic Neighborhood," SPACE, accessed August 15, 2022, https://www.space.com/19915-milky-way-galaxy.html.

making to others because it became crystal clear that *I was the problem.* Incredibly, when I took myself out of the way, the ceiling that had been limiting our company's profitability vaporized.

> *The Father that dwelleth in Me, He doeth the works.*
>
> **–JOHN 14:10**

I let go of believing that I knew best all on my own—how to run my company, how to be in relationships, how to take care of my body. I tapped into a greater mind, now guided to go along for the ride rather than steering the bus myself.

> *I had to stop playing God, learn to be myself, and join the team, where everyone helped each other succeed.*

I also had to quit believing and acting like I was the smartest person in the room, or that I should be. I decided to assume I was the dumbest person in the room, someone who needed help from others. I realized that I had two ears and one mouth for a reason, so I began talking less and listening more.

> *If you are the smartest person in the room, then you are in the wrong room.*
>
> **–RICHARD P. FEYNMAN**

THE PAUSE BUTTON

I created a "pause" button to change my habit of instant reactions, giving myself time to think so I could respond with empathy. This has saved my a** so many times! I'd like to have an actual button that reminds me to pause before I say something, before I hit SEND on a text or an email, before I make a decision. Something important happens in that moment, some kind of guidance shows up that I'd otherwise miss.

This is so important that I've adopted a new motto: "When in doubt … pause." And, to be totally truthful, I've learned to pause even when I feel swept up in certainty, when I'm not even questioning what I'm doing because I'm sure I'm right. That's the real danger zone because I'm blind to what I don't want to see that might rain on my parade.

Pausing can seem like being timid, but I learned that my partners and employees and family don't lose confidence in me when I pause for a moment to make sure of something. This has become an important new habit in my long journey towards becoming a better human, a better business man, and a better father to my four children.

Clemons is my oldest boy, and he probably took the biggest hit when I was out of it. I know I ruined his high school graduation. I probably robbed him of some of his childhood too because when I checked out, he had to step up and be the man of the house for a while, especially helping his mom.

Our reconciliation is a real joy in my life. I love it when he calls and says, "Hey. Can I come home and cook y'all steaks this weekend?" We're playing golf together again, a few weeks ago with his maternal grandfather, Cotton (who is an absolute trip)—three generations out there trying to hit that little white ball! Maybe our bond feels so special now because he did stand in for me, something I'll always be grateful for. Thankfully, we now have our family ordered the right way.

God gave me the great gift of showing me that I didn't need to take over from Clemons. We just naturally gave each other the gifts of becoming father, son, and best friend when the time was right. That's a gift that makes my heart overflow with gratitude.

He is definitely his father's son. I remember noticing him during a large, loud party once, huddled in a corner with some old man. I asked him afterward what was up with that. "Oh," he said, "the guy looked lonely, so I went over and hung out with him for a while. It was awkward at first, but turned out he was a pretty interesting guy." How many kids would do that at a party?

TIME-OUT

Prayer is for talking to God.
Meditation is for listening to God.

When you love someone, you want to spend time with them. Now I start every morning investing in my relationship with God.

God, the consuming fire, is not about burning you, but
about burning away everything that isn't you!

—RYAN STEVENSON

Before I begin my day, before I check email, before I do anything at all, I start with a time-out to focus on that primary relationship. I pray. I meditate. I sit in a quiet, private place where the dogs, the wife, and the kids can't disturb me. I often read from Just for Today, an online forum with inspirational quotes.

This puts me in touch with who I am, what's present without all the "doing." The investor Warren Buffett said, "I insist on a lot of time being spent, almost every day, to just sit and think. That is very uncommon in American business. I read and think. So, I do more reading and thinking, and make less impulse decisions than most people in business."

> I used to wake up with my hair on fire.
>
> I'd jump out of bed, into the shower, and rush out into the world.
>
> Every car was in my way, and I hurried to one meeting after another, each more stressful than the one before.

MORNING PRACTICE

You can develop your own morning routine, to nurture your relationship with God, however you perceive him/her/it, and to heal your father issues at the same time.

- O Breathe in and out slowly, deeply, and pause in between.

- O As you breathe in, think about your father. Picture him, smiling and happy. Every morning, love him a little bit more, just for being your dad.

- O As you breathe out, let your mind wander; think fondly about family, friends, and daily activities; and appreciate the opportunities you have to give value to others.

This practice keeps my father alive in me, without that shadow that was preventing me from being authentic. What I produce in my life carries his spirit and genetic markers, the same way I do and my children (his grandchildren) do. But I've disrupted and healed our father-son relationship by prioritizing my connection with a spiritual "father."

This gives new meaning to our paradox for this chapter: "Father is child to the man."

LESSONS LEARNED

- When my father died, I adopted his workaholic patterns, which almost killed me.
- The most important thing to me is to be authentic.
- No matter how successful I became, I felt unworthy because I didn't know who I was.
- When a doctor told me I had less than a month to live, I was forced to change.
- The remedy to our father issues is to connect with a higher power.
- I let go of trying to control my life.
- I remember to use my Pause Button.
- I begin each day with a time-out for prayer and contemplation.
- I love and respect my father, but I am my own authentic person.
- Father is child to the man.

NEXT:

What all authentic people feel called to do.

We Are the World

We are separate individuals, right?

Well ...

the earth also seems flat,
and the sun seems to revolve around the earth.

All is seldom as it seems.

We are individuals, and we are connected,
like waves in the ocean,

And we're designed to help each other.

CHAPTER THREE

Doing Good

*Our goal is to improve your health and quality of life with
kind, attentive service and easy access to our 30+ infusion
therapy centers throughout the Carolinas, Georgia, and
Alabama. We care for our patients like family ...*

—FROM OUR COMPANY WEBSITE, 2022.

*It's 2017. Our health care company is generating $80 million
in annual revenue with just eighty employees. But I barely know
any of them, I am out of touch with our three thousand patients,
and I am fighting with my business partners. We are successful
in spite of ourselves, and at some level, I am beginning to figure
out that I am the source of our problems.*

*I feel totally fraudulent, hiding the mess of my personal life
behind the surface appearance of professional success. I am Mr.
Self Sufficient, the Lone Ranger on steroids. This has to change.*

ALL OF US ARE HARDWIRED to help each other. So why do we
often wait for an emergency before we start doing that? In part,

because self-sufficiency is viewed as a positive value in our society. But as Associate Professor Todd Mei from the University of Dundee reports, "In a world in which each individual believes strongly in their own self-sufficiency, there is little room for genuine cooperation, only the fear that one self-sufficient being might be a threat to another."[18]

Our heroes? Self-sufficient individuals fighting with each other to win.

> *I had to learn the hard way that self-sufficiency is a dead end.*

Danielle, a blogger, wrote:

The myth of self-sufficiency runs deep, and it's a hard pill to swallow when you come to the realization that none of us have ever been completely self-sufficient. Not the settlers, not the Native Americans … no one. No man is an island, they say. And they're right.

We *all* rely upon community to some extent. Beyond just our family, we need other people. When they say it takes a village, in a lot of ways, it does. Native Americans, for instance, depended on everyone within their tribe to do their part. It wasn't just an individual, or an individual family. Settlers depended on community often when things needed done in a hurry, or when illness struck.

---

18   Todd Mei, "The Myth of Self-Sufficiency," Philosophy2U, September 13, 2021, https://www.philosophy2u.com/post/the-myth-of-self-sufficiency.

Our need for community is even more prevalent in today's modern world.[19]

This exposes another modern paradox: We've never been more connected, yet we feel alone. We can talk to each other, see each other, write to each other, send pictures and documents instantly across the wide world. We can join online communities, we can zoom with each other, we can like and dislike posts. But we've never felt lonelier. In fact, three out of five Americans today report feeling chronically lonely.[20] How can this be?

In every community, there is work to be done. In every nation, there are wounds to heal. In every heart, there is the power to do it.

—MARIANNE WILLIAMSON

I was trapped in solitary self-sufficiency by persistent feelings of unworthiness, all because I was comparing myself to others and, underneath it all, fearing that I had fallen too far for even God to love me anymore.

It didn't help that I was so seemingly successful in business. I knew what was really going on because my body was falling apart! I've since learned there are (at least) five reasons why we judge ourselves against others, rather than simply being our unique selves.

1. *The Power of Outside Influences.*

We are bombarded by a constant media stream that either

---

19   Danielle McCoy, "The Myth of Self-Sufficiency," The Rustic Elk, July 29, 2022, https://www.therusticelk.com/the-myth-of-self-sufficiency/.

20   Elena Renken, "Most Americans Are Lonely, and Our Workplace Culture May Not Be Helping," NPR, January 23, 2020, https://www.npr.org/sections/health-shots/2020/01/23/798676465/most-americans-are-lonely-and-our-workplace-culture-may-not-be-helping.

overtly or subtly defines what is "normal" or "best." We are urged to compare ourselves to others and then buy something in order to become better or achieve more.

2. *There's Only One Right Way.*

We see this belief reinforced by experts who instantly clap back their answer to questions that deserve more thought, maybe even an honest "I don't know." The message? Feeling uncertain? There must be something wrong with me.

3. *I Must Always Win.*

Our modern and historical heroes—real and screen sized—always win. Shouldn't we? James Bond. Florence Nightingale, Jason Bourne. Wonder Woman. Superman. They prevail over impossible obstacles to win—no matter what. Persistence is a badge of honor. It's the loser who surrenders.

4. *Asking for Help Is a Sign of Weakness.*

We hesitate to portray ourselves as needy or incompetent. We fear being devalued or even shunned if we dare admit that we aren't self-sufficient.

5. *We Are Separate.*

Four hundred years ago, the English poet John Donne wrote, "No man is an island," but the opposite belief persists. Hey, even islands are connected, and nature is an orchestra. Trees root in soil containing millions of life forms that cocreate a healthy forest together.

"You have great potential!"

This is the worst thing a person can hear if there's no guidance to help them develop it. But it's the *best* thing they can hear when that guidance *is* available. Imagine that becoming standard fare for young people. I'm sure that would help alleviate the anxiety that eventually contributes to self-harm. But it would need to prioritize being over doing, so they could avoid my fake success crash and become fully authentic, being themselves, and doing what they love.

> *Let yourself be silently drawn by the strange pull of*
> *what you really love. It will not lead you astray.*
>
> **—RUMI**

ORIGINS

We can look back to our childhood to learn where our personal version of self-sufficiency originated, why we became inauthentic, and why we live our lives and run our businesses the way we do.

Both my parents worked all the time, so that's what I learned to do. Copying them also programmed me to strive hard for approving attention and recognition.

My parents met when my mother was fourteen, and he was the only man she ever dated. They were about as close as any couple could be. She was an accomplished breadwinner in her own right, working right alongside my dad. Besides doing the business accounting, she kept house and raised us four kids. Mom built my dad, and he built everything else.

When Dad died, she withdrew. She'd supported my father all her adult life, and now she just dropped everything and turned the businesses over to the children. She left the family home, she stopped cooking, she didn't date, and she didn't entertain. But she *did* develop a beautifully interdependent relationship with her sister. They lived their best lives together for years.

Today, she's back on top of the world. My sister Christy and I have lunch with her five days a week, and our other sister, Gina—who lives three hours away—talks with her on the phone three or four times every day. We love our mother and admire the changes she's made. It's blessed our whole family and the community we live in. The choices she's made have helped me resolve some of that early programming.

> *Our brains are wired for connection, but trauma*
> *rewires them for protection. That's why healthy*
> *relationships are difficult for wounded people.*
> **—RYAN NORTH**

Obviously, I didn't intend to hurt the ones I loved. None of us do. But our early programming can alienate us from others, and it's difficult to change those deeply ingrained patterns. I needed help to heal and overcome that programming.

Ron Welchel, our director of HR, knew just the person, a business consultant named Sharon Randaccio. Sharon is a Business First "40 under 40" award winner and a recipient of the "Women of Influence" honor. She received the Distinguished Alumni Award from SUNY Buffalo and the "Woman of Distinction" award from the Amherst Chamber of Commerce. Her bio says, "She asks the tough questions and helps clients drive transformation."

Sharon did just that for our organization and for me, as my personal performance coach. Our collaboration became one of the most fruitful experiences of my professional life. I could never have made such a fundamental change to my operating system on my own. Sharon helped me change direction.

If you don't change direction, you may end up where you are headed.

—LAO TSU

Changing direction is hard. But Lao Tsu also said, "The journey of a thousand miles begins with a single step." Sharon helped me take that first step, then the next one, and the next one, until I was firmly established on a new path.

For instance, I routinely took an interest in the personal lives of our employees, at least the ones I had contact with. But I didn't offer them the help they needed at work. I just assumed everybody could and would handle what they needed to. So I had these great friendships with people who were struggling on the job. It wasn't enough to be a nice boss; I had to learn how to help them shine.

WE ARE THE WORLD

Pride can get in the way when we try to change direction or collaborate on a team. When the producer Quincy Jones welcomed celebrity singers to the first recording session for "We Are the World," he famously told them: "Check your egos at the door."

American singer Harry Belafonte came up with this idea in 1985. He created USA for Africa, a nonprofit organization to fight famine in Africa. Forty-six of the world's best musicians joined together to perform the song, which won three Grammy Awards, sold twenty million copies, raised $63 million, and inspired a series of similar social benefit initiatives including Live Aid, Farm Aid, and Tsunami Aid.

> *We are the world,*
>
> *we are the children*
>
> *we are the ones who make a brighter day,*
>
> *so let's start giving.*
>
> *There's a choice we're making,*
>
> *we're saving our own lives,*
>
> *it's true we'll make a better day, just you and me.* [21]

The song inspired many millions of people everywhere, and this particular lyric describes the early days of my journey: "There comes a time when we heed a certain call." I heard a call, but I sure took my time to answer it! Another lyric says, "We can't go on pretending day-by-day." Well, I did my best there, locked in stubborn denial about my health, my marriage, my business, and the lack of meaning in my life.

How 'bout a shot of truth in that denial cocktail.

—JENNIFER SALAIZ

"Let's start giving" might be my favorite line in that song. This is the key. There are no preconditions! It's just "Let's start giving." In the final analysis, our lives have meaning because of how we help

---

21   "We Are the World," Wikipedia, accessed August 29, 2022, https://en.wikipedia.org/wiki/We_Are_the_World.

others. That's the real reason we should look after ourselves, so we can continue to help our families and businesses and communities and the world at large.

LESSONS FROM HARRIET

Harriet Tubman is a prominent figure from American history who exemplified selfless giving. Harriet was born in Maryland in 1820. She escaped her enslavement on a plantation and used the Underground Railroad to lead hundreds of other slaves to freedom before the Civil War.

When Harriet was just twelve, she threw herself in the way of a heavy weight that a slave owner hurled at a fugitive. It struck Harriet's head, leaving her with permanent injuries that resulted in headaches and narcolepsy, a condition that caused her to fall asleep at random moments. These symptoms persisted the rest of her long life but didn't interfere with a life of selfless service to others.

I had crossed the line. I was free; but there was no one to welcome me to the land of freedom. I was a stranger in a strange land.

—HARRIET TUBMAN

In 1861, when the Civil War broke out, she helped fugitives at Fort Monroe and helped treat sick soldiers. In 1863, she joined a Union army spy network and provided intelligence about enemy supply routes and troops.

After the Civil War, she moved to New York. She never learned to read or write but spoke on behalf of the women's suffrage movement. In 1896, Harriet bought nearby land and developed the Harriet Tubman Home for Aged and Indigent Colored People. Her health deteriorated, and she moved into her own rest home in 1911. She died of pneumonia in 1913.

She has been well remembered. A score of schools and museums bear her name. Her story has been told in books, movies, and documentaries, and a ship is named after her, the SS *Harriet Tubman*. In 2016, the US Treasury announced an upcoming $20 bill that will feature Harriet's image, rather than former president and slaveowner Andrew Jackson.[22]

Gaining her own physical freedom was just the beginning for Harriet. Being free while others remained in slavery compelled her to do whatever she could to free them. This included being shot at while living as a fugitive with a bounty on her head. Helping to free others, she freed herself more completely.

Her story raises the bar for us all. While the media continues to overwhelm us with dark stories of disasters and impending disasters, the fact is that millions of ordinary people are helping others in extraordinary ways. For instance, David Flucker lives in Edinburg and commutes four hours, three days a week to volunteer at a hospice. He's one hundred years old!

No matter what our personal limitations might be, we can "just start giving."

Ordinary people everywhere are doing extraordinary things for others.

THE BLESSING OF GRIEF

Grief is not my favorite emotion. I've suffered from depression, so I know the deadening effect it can exert. But I've come to understand

---

22   History.com editors, "Harriet Tubman," History, January 26, 2022, https://www.history.com/topics/black-history/harriet-tubman.

the difference between depression (an illness), and sorrow, which has a place in our lives. In fact, since we all suffer and feel sad at times, this can be a way to connect with other people.

The darker the night, the brighter the stars,
The deeper the grief, the closer is God!
—APOLLON MAYKOV

Like most of you, I've had virtually no education about how to handle sadness. I did learn that there's a difference between *feeling* sad and *being* sad. We can feel something without being totally controlled by it. I know depression is real and sometimes requires treatment. But grief is unavoidable; it's a natural part of life.

When I suffer, I remember that others are suffering too, probably in worse ways than I am. We had a hurricane here recently. We lost two docks and had four feet of water in our house. Bad news, right? Well, sure, but we have two beach houses. That means we are far better off than most people, at least financially.

I began to understand that suffering and disappointments and melancholy are there not to vex us or cheapen us or deprive us of our dignity but to mature and transfigure us.
—HERMANN HESSE

Instead of getting into self-pity about our situation, I thought about a friend with a child who is dying. His burden is so much greater than mine. I reached out to him to see if I could help. When I get over myself and try to help someone else, my own suffering doesn't seem so bad.

EMPOWERING FRIENDSHIPS

A friend's mentor once advised him that people either lift you up or pull you down. Darren Hardy, writing in *The Compound Effect*, said: "According to research by social psychologist Dr. David McClelland of Harvard, [the people you habitually associate with] determine as much as 95 percent of your success or failure in life."[23]

People either lift you up or pull you down.

Maybe we should view our relationships through this lens. Here's a simple way to do that right now. Draw a vertical line down the middle of the page and begin listing your closest family members, business associates, and friends on either side. You can write into this space or use a separate piece of paper. Title the left column FANS. It's for anyone who is supporting you to become a better person. Title the right column PARTY POOPERS, recording the names of anyone holding you where you are or dragging you down.

FANS	PARTY POOPERS

---

23   Darren Hardy, *The Compound Effect* (New York: Hachette Books, 2020), 127.

Now circle the five names of those you spend the most time with. Make sure you choose from both your personal and professional life. As inspirational speaker Jim Rohn says, "You are the average of the five people you spend the most time with." When you study these five names, ask yourself: "What does he/she contribute to my life?"

> *We cannot control a relationship. We can only contribute*
> *to a relationship. All relationships, business or personal,*
> *are an opportunity to serve another human being.*
> **—SIMON SINEK**

Here comes the challenging part: what will you do with what you just learned? Will you choose to spend more time with those who support your ongoing positive growth? You might look at your list again and circle different names.

> *No amount of personal will power is enough*
> *to change your personal habits all on your own.*

We need trusted friends and allies who will support us to sustain our commitment to travel in a new direction. We need them most when we're tempted to revert back to familiar, comfortable habits, and those moments inevitably come.

Surround yourself with friends who hold you to the highest level of personal integrity. Choose people who are servant leaders, selfless and generous.

EVENING REVIEW

In chapter one, I told you about my regular morning time-out, investing in my relationship with God. I end the day with an honest review of what happened.

Sometimes I journal; sometimes I just think back over the day, recalling whatever stands out. To simplify and focus this review process, I ask myself a few guiding questions, like:

1. Was I being completely authentic in every situation?

2. Was I controlling or collaborating?

3. Was I an empathetic friend?

4. Was I a servant leader?

5. Did I misrepresent myself or force an issue?

6. What did I learn?

7. What can I celebrate about today?

Create your own Q&A to learn, celebrate, and fully complete the day.

Our paradox under discussion is "We are the world." As Herman Melville wrote, "We cannot live only for ourselves. A thousand fibers connect us with our fellow men; and among those fibers, as sympathetic threads, our actions run as causes, and they come back to us as effects."

Melville reveals a great secret. Our life experience is not imposed upon us. We are always creating it, and much of what we come to experience is the result of our relationships. When we start treating others as we wish to be treated ourselves (that sounds familiar), the reflections change.

LESSONS LEARNED

- Self-sufficiency is a myth. We need each other.
- We learn our management strategies from our early family experiences.
- I needed help to change my operating system and make letting go my new normal.
- We are happiest when we are helping others.
- Empowering friendships support us to become our authentic selves.
- A regular evening review helps us learn from the day and calm our minds before sleep.
- We are the world.

NEXT:

What about the bottom line?

Profit before Profit

Profit results from work, ingenuity, sometimes luck, right?

Well …

what if doing well is a reflection of doing good?

*Putting social profit first (people and environment),
results in financial profit without harmful side effects,
but only when we're synchronized
with the full-profit system known as nature.*

*Life is a profitable enterprise
when everything and everyone wins.*

CHAPTER FOUR

Doing Well

The journey of building a great business is not about the destination at all. Of course, you want it to be highly profitable and generate wealth for yourself and others. Yet, along the way, you need to enjoy the lives that you'll touch. You need to get excited about the value you'll create for customers, enjoy the pure pleasure of playing the game of business, and be able to take pride in the self-perpetuating system you've built.

—GINO WICKMAN, *TRACTION*

It's September 11, 2001, exactly one month after my dad died. I'm twenty-eight and suddenly the CEO of Winyah Healthcare Group, a collection of all our family companies. I start meeting with business brokers and VC firms (venture capitalists). Several competitors have begun telling our customers and referral sources that we will fail without the leadership and financing from my father. Now, here's the ideal role for me. I can rise to the occasion and be the hero. I can finally make my dad proud. But he won't be here to see it, and that haunts me.

I wake up that morning with a hangover. As I struggle through my fog and pick at an omelet, I see the news coming out of New York. A plane has flown into the World Trade Center. I drop everything and race between our home health care offices. None of them have TVs so I buy TVs and connect them. Fifty of us huddle together in the Columbia, South Carolina, office, frozen in silence. Later, I sit in my hotel room, wondering: Trouble often comes in threes. My father has died, the terrorists have struck—what's next?

Bank of America had been our lender for a long time, and our usual banker had become a personal friend. A few days later, we had visitors from B of A, but none of them were that guy. Playing my hero role, I projected confidence and welcomed them with open arms and humor. But they were there to deliver bad news. Bank of America called my loans, my partners' loans, and all of my Dad's loans as well. We're talking about many millions of dollars and a ridiculously few days to find it. I was twenty-eight years old, married, with two small children. My hero role just got a lot more challenging. In fact, I felt helpless.

It always seems impossible until it's done.

—NELSON MANDELA

The bank called those loans because my Dad was gone, but also because we had zero infrastructure. I could blame my father, I could blame myself, I could blame our founding partners. But the fact was that we had zero support in HR, accounting, payroll, AP, and reimbursement and collections; no audit or the ability to do one; and virtually no management team for a $25 million revenue company. I picked up the phone and asked for help from two friends who had always been there for me. I also called a gentleman my father introduced me to just twenty-four hours before he died. That was no accident!

We met the bank's ninety-day deadline, and these new colleagues helped me get the company completely refinanced. One of them joined our company, and the other joined another bank. We're still with that bank, twenty-one years later.

The moral to this episode? We never do things alone, especially heroic things. I can take some of the credit because I played a key role. But I was part of a cast that included many heroes. Together, we got over that hurdle, the first of many on the road ahead.

The trouble with success like that is that it's addictive. Sure, that episode ended well, but it fortified my belief in driving hard and never giving up. Surrender and win? If you'd mentioned those two words in the same sentence to me back then, I would have laughed out loud. I had some hard learning to do.

I began speeding toward the on-ramp for the fast lane,
recklessly out of control. I'd stay there for the next ten years.

LIFE IN THE FAST LANE

As I walked into one of the tallest buildings in downtown Atlanta and entered the law offices of Alston and Bird, one of the most prestigious law firms in the Southeast, I remembered a moment in grad school when I realized what I wanted to do when I grew up. I wanted to be "fancy." Now, here I was in this fancy building doing fancy things.

When one lives attached to money,
pride, or power, it is impossible to be truly happy.
—POPE FRANCIS

Meanwhile, I was driving a Buick Regal instead of flying private, my company was barely surviving, and we were spending more on legal fees than we had in the bank. But we were swinging for the fences, and failure was not an option. My partner and I had to get a group of partnerships and valuations done, with everyone comfortable enough to move forward. I was playing my part, and my partners and family were trusting me.

We pulled it off.

That was the day I felt like a big shot. It was also the day I began comparing myself to the others playing this same game. I entered the M&A (mergers and acquisitions) world, which was far different from being an operator. They don't teach you about this stuff when you get your master's of health administration. I began hearing about multiples of EBITDA (earnings before interest, tax, depreciation, and amortization), which is how companies are valued. I learned that companies had to have infrastructure in order to make it to the next level.

I was getting a PhD in M&A, but it was probably the most expensive way to get one, learning through my mistakes. That proved costly. We had to dine with bankers, accounting firms, PE firms, investment bankers, companies we wanted to buy and companies that wanted to buy us, companies that wanted to sell us stuff, and companies that we wanted to buy stuff from. Meanwhile, we had our own company to run.

I was invited to join a group called the Home Care 100. I did my homework, and it began to pay off. We became the prettiest girl at the party, and everyone wanted to dance with us. That is, everyone wanted to buy our home health care company. Most business owners would be flattered by this. I wasn't, because I had the disease of "more."

*George Orwell said that to see what's in front of
your nose requires a constant struggle.*

—MARK MANSON

I wanted to be the acquirer, not the one being acquired.

Two companies like ours emerged as the Big Two in America. The
leaders became, and still are, my friends. But I wanted to be them.
I wanted the pats on the head they were getting. I wanted to be the
good son who made his dad proud, to do even better than his dad.
Mine would have enjoyed that.

He'd been grooming me from birth. He honestly hoped that
I'd become governor one day. And we wanted to become a publicly
traded company. That's what we had made up our minds to do, and
it didn't matter that he wasn't around anymore; I'd make it happen
myself.

However, I'd forgotten a few things: our loans had been called,
and I had payroll of $500,000 to meet on Friday with no money in
the bank. We were literally holding our breath and praying. "Please,
God, don't let those checks clear until next Friday." Looking back,
it seems insane, but twenty-eight-year-old Gary believed with total
conviction that he and his team deserved a seat at that table.

We put together a plan. All the leaders of our company would
receive a fat check if we got bigger or if we sold. I created equity for
those leaders, and we set off on a growth campaign. We also aimed
for new targets like EBITDA, which I'd been learning about over all
those dinners. It began to work. We turned several of our divisions
around rapidly by sharing the wealth with our leaders. My father had
grown up on a sharecropping farm, so we called this business model
"sharecropping." It worked.

DOING WELL

This introduces the third component of the Success Paradox Lifestyle (SPL): doing well. That is, being financially profitable.

We make a living by what we get. We make a life by what we give.

—WINSTON CHURCHILL

We continued to grow our companies and enjoyed great success. I was runner-up in the Ernst and Young Entrepreneur Award twice, we sold one company for $12 million, one for $20 million, started another company and sold it in four years for $20 million, sold another company for $18 million, started another one and sold it for $8 million, and bought back a company that we sold for $18 million for $1.2 million. Plus, we turned our first offer of $16 million—made just months after my dad died—into $78 million in ten years. We also created thousands of jobs, and many of those jobs still exist today, filled by the same employees. The company we bought back and built is now the largest company of its kind in America.

I have the same partners today that I had when my father died.

So, what's the problem with this picture? Along the way, I got lost.

I got lost in the politics of business, the stress of life, workaholism, and living out of balance. I forgot what was important. I kept comparing my performance to others and believing that selling our companies (at significant profits) meant failure. I forgot to be grateful. I forgot why I was in business. And I forgot this childhood memory:

I'm tagging along with my father as we tour rural South Carolina nursing homes. I peer through open doors where desperate grandmothers are tied down in their beds, begging and pleading, "Please, help me!"

I'm in grad school, wondering what I want to be when I grow up. Right there, I decide that I want to keep people out of nursing homes and hospitals by helping them get the medicine and care they need, right in their own homes.

The vision for Palmetto Infusion is born.

That vision got lost when I began what I call "chasing." Chasing is pursuing what the world tells us success is rather than what our inner voice tells us. I became deaf to that voice, but I got financially rewarded for the phony success that followed. Of course, it was never enough.

I believed the business books I was reading, that obstacles were to be overcome with more hard work. Never quit, right? That "push over the goal line" mentality was deeply ingrained in my work ethic.

If I made $2 million on a business deal, I would rush out to spend $3 million on the next deal, without considering taxes or even talking to my wife. Then, instead of getting respect from her, a pat on the back, an "Atta boy for a job well done," I got a "Who cares?" or "When can we go to Disney World?"

I had no idea that I was responsible for triggering those reactions. I know now, but at the time, those remarks sent me into what my pastor calls the "dance." This is a dynamic where a wife withholds respect while the husband withholds love, and this repeats until one of them breaks the cycle. My wife and I played this all the way to the War of the Roses!

It was normal for me to work fifteen hours or more a day Monday through Friday. I didn't fish, hunt, play golf, keep up with friends, or do anything socially that wasn't related to work.

I was defining what it meant to be a workaholic.

BEYOND THE POINT OF NO RETURN

When swimming into a dark tunnel, there arrives a point of no return when you no longer have enough breath to double back. Your choice is to swim forward into the unknown ... and pray for an exit.

—DAN BROWN

It's April 18, 2017. I've screwed up big time, and it's the last straw for my wife. She orders me out of the house and forbids me any further contact with our kids.

I drive myself to a nearby hotel and drink myself blind, about a half gallon of vodka every day for three days, without eating a thing. When I start bleeding, I drive myself to the hospital. My doctor informs me that I probably have less than a month to live. This gets my attention.

My friend Mark shows up with enough tough love to jolt me from self-pity into rehab, which is horrible. I persevere, and my wife takes me back, but there's no quick fairy-tale ending to my struggles. I'm living with pain in my back and right side, and my overall health continues to deteriorate.

I finally begin to address my mental health ... by taking care of my physical health. I'm still recovering from one back surgery and two hip replacements when I find out that I have to go back under the knife for another hip replacement because one of my new hips became infected. With the support of God, my wife, and a new mental outlook, I make it through that last surgery and recover with Advil as my only pain med, and definitely without alcohol. Within six weeks I'm flying to Ecuador and Galapagos to visit our daughter.

I'd spent decades trying to be a really good guy, addicted to self-sufficiency and alcohol. Well, that made me a really bad guy. Now, being honest, vulnerable, and overcoming the fear of asking for help (doing the opposite), I find myself reunited with my entire family, standing on the equator for the first time in my life, atop one of the tallest cities in the Americas.

I'd say all that ranks as something of a miracle.

I needed more help. I reached out to a doctor, a surgeon, to my friend Mark, my wife, my kids, and my business partners. The tide of loving understanding that came flooding back to me burst my bubble of self-sufficiency.

My arrogant self-sufficiency faded away, and I experienced something I hadn't felt in ages: humility.

This was a big turning point. But life didn't suddenly become a feel-good walk in the park. I'd quit drinking (and have remained sober since that day). I began changing personal habits and repairing relationships. But I didn't know who I really was, and I had no clue how my personal changes could ever translate into business success. I had to figure that out as I went along, exploring totally unknown territory.

I discovered what I now call "relaxed productivity." Now I don't *make* anything happen; I *let* things happen. This would only be faintly interesting were it not for the phenomenal business success I've achieved since that turning point, not by working hard or getting lucky but by surrendering control.

> Now I don't *make* anything happen; I *let* things happen.

Surrender and win? That's not just a catchy subtitle for our book. I'm living this paradox every day. I do the opposite of what I used to do. And … it's highly profitable!

> *Look at what the majority of people are doing,*
> *and do the exact opposite.*
>
> **—EARL NIGHTINGALE**

REIMAGINING THE BOTTOM LINE

In 1994, John Elkington, founder of the management consultancy SustainAbility, coined the term Triple Bottom Line (TBL). This redefined business success to include social, environmental, and economic profit. Although TBL was conceived to encourage a reconsideration of capitalism itself and has been widely implemented, Elkington recently recommended recalling the concept.

He wrote, "Whereas CEOs, CFOs, and other corporate leaders move heaven and earth to ensure that they hit their profit targets, the same is very rarely true of their people and planet targets. Clearly, the Triple Bottom Line has failed to bury the single bottom line paradigm."[24]

---

24   John Elkington, "25 Years Ago I Coined the Phrase 'Triple Bottom Line.' Here's Why It's Time to Rethink It," *Harvard Business Review*, June 25, 2018, https://hbr. org/2018/06/25-years-ago-i-coined-the-phrase-triple-bottom-line-heres-why-im-giving-up-on-it.

Elkington explained why this way: "To truly shift the needle ... we need a new wave of TBL innovation and deployment." He followed up by warning that even this would likely not be enough. I agree. And I propose that, for TBL to become more than greenwashing, a new priority is needed. Can you guess what it is? Giving up.

As Patricia Haddock writes, "It takes courage and maturity to admit that we're on the wrong path, in the wrong place, or with the wrong person. Walking away is an act of self-care. It's an assertion that meeting our needs, finding happiness, and upholding our core values are more important than the situation we are in. We're putting ourselves first. This isn't selfish; it's survival. Staying too long when we should leave is running in the same place, hoping to get somewhere else. Instead, we're digging a deeper and deeper rut. The time comes when we have to make the hard decision to give up, climb out, and walk away."

Elkington realized that his noble concept isn't cutting it, and he's saying so loud and clear. I wonder, as he did, will anything change by continuing to try? Or, how about giving up?

A NEW MODEL

For-profit corporations increase share value for stockholders. Nonprofit organizations create social value. Some companies, like ours, manage to do both. We're experimenting with a new model, what we call "full-profit." It's all about the profit generating power of generosity.

For instance, our CEO, David Goodall, has instituted a policy of spot bonuses. Every center director is authorized to gift employees up to 1 percent of their operation's gross payroll. They don't need permission to do this; it's their call. This incentivizes everyone and creates a super-fun working environment. Because the decisions are made at the local level, it furthers our goal of making a large company feel small.

For it is in giving that we receive.

—ST. FRANCIS OF ASSISI

Since we're not taught to be generous with our money, we need to be deliberate to change our thinking and behaviors. Here are a few practices to experiment with:

- Tithing. You don't have to belong to a church to donate. Decide what percentage of your monthly income you want to give away—no strings attached—commit, and do it … at the beginning, not the end, of each month.

- Write "Thank you" on your checks or attach a note with online payments. As you do, focus appreciation for what you're paying for.

- Pay for someone else. Like the car behind you in the toll line. Or pick up a stranger's tab in a coffee shop, because you noticed something special about someone at a nearby table.

- Jackpot tipping. Decide to tip with cash and choose a standard percentage. When service is substandard, tip less, but put the difference in a special place in your purse or wallet. When the service is outstanding, give your server everything in there. This means you might tip $30 for a coffee. Your server just hit the jackpot!

Everything changes when we prioritize being authentic, which inspires us to help others, and results in doing well. We create a fundamentally different kind of profit: a reflection of our goodwill. Imagine more and more individuals shifting their relationship with money and making their companies full-profit enterprises, putting profit (people and social) before profit (financial). They would do good, and they would do well. Profit is a reflection of doing good.

Imagine you're living in Biblical times. You follow Jesus to a remote location in the desert with a crowd. It's a hot day, and you're not sure how long you'll be out there, so you probably brought something to drink and eat. As Jesus speaks, your heart opens, and you're inspired to share what you brought with others, and so are they. There is plenty for all.

Now, there's a different interpretation of the loaves and fishes parable!

The paradox here in chapter four is "profit before profit." Beyond the confusing play on words, the meaning relates to prioritizing social/people profit before financial profit. But it's not an either/or. There are for-profit corporations and nonprofit organizations; we advocate for full-profit ventures of every kind where money flows freely and everyone enjoys abundance.

SHIFTING GEARS

It's time to roll up our sleeves and get to work. Part Two will be your personal workbook, designed to help you learn, adopt, practice, and integrate the Success Paradox Lifestyle (SPL), to transform your personal life, companies, families, and communities into environments that support everyone to surrender and win.

Let's establish your starting point. For each statement below, check the appropriate box from 1 to 5: 1 for strongly no, 5 for absolutely yes, 2–4 for degrees in between. Trust your first intuitive answer.

	1	2	3	4	5
Having read these four chapters, I feel engaged and ready to learn/change.					
I feel genuine remorse for some of my past behaviors.					
I am ready to surrender willpower for willingness.					
Discovering and being who I am is my top priority.					
I understand why "doing good" must come before "doing well."					
Nurturing my family experience is as important as developing my career.					
I know that I need help and am willing to ask for it.					
I enjoy helping others any way I can.					
Creating financial profit is an essential ingredient in success, but is not the first priority.					
I understand what it means to surrender and win and am ready to experience what that means more fully.					

Total your scores and multiply by two to determine your percentage score.

SCORING RESULTS (%)

20-34   Having a Success Paradox Buddy to work with will help you do the initial heavy lifting.

35-50   Keeping a Success Paradox Journal will help you self-regulate.

51-66   Consulting the Resource section on our website will help accelerate your progress.

67-82   You are ready to provide leadership in your organization/ family.

83-100   Coaching others may become an option for you.

Visit successparadoxbook.com to access guidance on these categories from our website.

LESSONS LEARNED

- We never do things alone, especially heroic things.
- Life in the fast lane wears you out.
- Success can feel like failure when you don't know who you are.
- I let go of willpower and became willing to change my ways.
- My turning point came when I finally admitted I needed help and reached out.
- Compassion is our best motivator.
- Profit before profit.

NEXT:

Part Two begins your own journey into The Success Paradox Lifestyle (SPL).

*Transformation is a process,
and as life happens there are tons
of ups and downs.
It's a journey of discovery—there
are moments on mountaintops and
moments in deep valleys of despair.*

— RICK WARREN

PART TWO

The journey of the hero is about the courage to seek the depths; the image of creative rebirth; the eternal cycle of change within us; the uncanny discovery that the seeker is the mystery which the seeker seeks to know.

The hero journey is a symbol that binds, in the original sense of the word, two distant ideas, the spiritual quest of the ancients with the modern search for identity ...

—JOSEPH CAMPBELL

You Can't Get Here from There

You can't get there from here, right?
(We've heard that joke.)

Well …

switch it around.

What if "here," our best possible experience,
is actually our natural inner state?

"Here" is already here.
Are we here to fully enjoy it?

CHAPTER FIVE

Finding Your Why

Man has gone out to explore other worlds and other civilizations without having explored his own labyrinth of dark passages and secret chambers, and without finding what lies behind doorways that he himself has sealed.

—STANISŁAW LEM

HOW WAS I ABLE TO AVOID BANKRUPTCY at age twenty-eight when my father suddenly died, leaving me as the primary owner (and suddenly CEO) of a company with about 500 full- or part-time employees and virtually no infrastructure? I already mentioned that two months after my Dad's funeral, the bank called all our loans, giving me ninety days to raise $30 million.

How did I turn my health around after a doctor told me, "Gary, you've probably got less than a month to live"? How did I quit drinking, stop comparing myself to others, escape the trap of workaholism, and heal my family relationships?

How did we create a team that took a company valued at $20 million and increase its valuation to almost $400 million in just five years, expanding our work force from eighty to five hundred while gaining eight thousand customers, with consistently high satisfaction ratings from both employees and customers on regular surveys?

I surrendered. I let go. I got out of the way.
I turned my life over to a higher power.

I exchanged willpower for willingness. I actually *let* that higher power run my life. I prioritized being authentic, doing good, and doing well. I've lived by this code ever since.

You may not be faced with anything like the apocalypse that almost obliterated me (I hope not!), but you've got your own challenges, or you wouldn't still be reading. Others more fortunate may already enjoy a stable, successful situation. But if *you're* still reading, you know there's more, and you want it.

Every issue you face is going to have its own set of challenges.
—PATRICK BET-DAVID

While I understood the value of business skills and invested heavily in honing my trade, creating an image of success for all the world to see, I didn't know that upgrades were also available for my "living life" skills. Like so many of us, I was putting the cart before the horse. I would borrow money, leverage myself, use credit cards, and of course work harder, but I always wanted things before I had earned them. I've since learned that true success builds on the foundation of our true character. I was tired of being a character rather than having character! "Being" is as important as "doing," and it comes first. The six chapters here in Part Two will help you construct your foundation.

BEFORE WE START

Remember heading out on a road trip? What happened before you took off?

You had a destination. You looked at a map or set your GPS. If you'd never been there before and the journey was risky—like climbing Everest or visiting your mother-in-law (just kidding!)—you hired a guide. You gathered supplies, everything you might need on the trip.

But there's something else you did that's even more important. I'll explain with a brief story:

A boy scout returned to headquarters with his uniform in tatters, bruised and bleeding. "What happened to you?" asked the scoutmaster.

"I helped an old lady across the street," the boy replied, nursing his bloody lip.

"But why are you all banged up like this?"

"She didn't want to go!"

Do you want to go? Is this a journey you really want to take? There are plenty of excellent business books out there, many of which I've read and continue to find valuable, even essential to my business success. If all you want is *business* success, then I recommend you close this book and read those. I'm not going to hustle you across a street you don't want to cross!

You cannot achieve a new outcome without learning something new and practicing what you learned (probably outside your comfort zone).

—KEITH J. CUNNINGHAM

If you *do* want more; if you want peace, to feel like you're living your own life; if you want to truly enjoy your success and sleep well at night; if you feel ready to explore the actual details of what that would look like to surrender and win in your life and your organization, then you're *almost* ready to rock and roll. But first, you have to find your why.

Why do you want to go down this road and not some other? In *Start with Why*, Simon Sinek wrote: "Very few people or companies can clearly articulate why they do what they do. When I say why, I don't mean to make money—that's a result. By why I mean what is your purpose, cause or belief? why does your company exist? why do you get out of bed every morning?"[25]

Finding my "why" had a lot to do with that young boy who killed himself. His tragedy jolted me to my core. In an instant I knew that I wouldn't be able to live with myself if I didn't dedicate the rest of my life to helping others like Jack, not just teenagers but anyone who is on that great hairy edge of giving up on life. I went right up to that edge myself, but I survived. Was that just for my personal benefit? Absolutely not. That experience triggered in me what's natural to us all, the deep desire to help others.

It's the Harriet Tubman dynamic. She couldn't rest, just being free herself. She had to go back for others. You have a "why," a personal calling connected to helping people. It already lives within you, but you may not know it fully yet. Everything in this book is offered to help you find it and live it.

> *There is no exercise better for the heart than*
> *reaching down and lifting people up.*
>
> **—JOHN HOLMES**

---

25   Simon Sinek, *Start with Why* (New York: Penguin, 2009), 39.

What breaks your heart?
Finding out will lead you to your why.

FINDING YOUR WHY QUESTIONNAIRE

You can fill this out right here or access the form at successparadox-book.com.

For each statement below, check the appropriate box from 1 to 5: 1 for strongly no, 5 for absolutely yes, 2–4 for degrees in between. Trust your first intuitive answer.

	1	2	3	4	5
I know why I get out of bed each morning and can't wait for the day to start.					
I love what I'm doing and have identified my contribution to the world, for now.					
I am organizing my life and career to make this "why" my top priority.					
I am actively engaging others to help me do this.					

Total your scores and multiply by four. Redoing this questionnaire periodically will help ensure you are heading in the right direction. Journaling is also important, to track the evolution of your awareness.

DATE: _____   SCORE: _____

0-25 You don't know, and you don't know that you don't know. This is a perfect starting point … if you break inertia by taking one step forward.

26-50   You don't know, and you *know* that you don't know. It's a humbling moment. Use meditative time to increase your intuitive knowing.

51-75   You know, but you don't know that you know. You're primed and ready to actively engage with this learning journey.

76-100   You know, and you *know* that you know. You know your why. This book and other resources can help you fulfil your calling and connect you with fellow travelers on this path.

FIRST THINGS FIRST

I surrendered. Not because I thought it would help me win. I didn't know that concept yet. The strategy, "surrender and win" developed as we wrote this book. Back then, I had no other choice. You're probably not dangling at the end of the vine the way I was. So without that life-or-death pressure I was under, what could motivate you to make such a paradoxical shift? It's going to take a personally transformative experience, not just information. I'll do my best to set this up for you right here, right now.

My own deepest learning happens through listening. For those who share my learning style, we've created short audio programs, accessible through our website, successparadoxbook.com. You may learn visually or kinesthetically, but most of us can be moved by evocative listening presentations that invite us to stop thinking and feel.

Visit our site successparadoxbook.com to find a guided audio meditation on Finding Your Why. Here's the text for the audio simulation. Pause frequently as you read/listen, so you can drop deep below the superficial concerns in your life.

Imagine an ocean.
There are waves on the surface,
but underneath it's calm.
Let's go there.

Find a quiet, private space, settle into a comfortable chair, and close your eyes (if you're listening). Take a couple of deep breaths and notice the tension flooding out of your body.

Let your mind wander. Enjoy watching your thoughts and letting them go, just floating in and out. Feel what it's like to be present, here, reading these words or listening to them. There's nothing to achieve, nothing to prove, no problem to solve … you're just being, being alive.

Now imagine the screen of your mind going blank. Thoughts still come and go, but they seem almost invisible. The space is more noticeable. Now, into this space, welcome a feeling. It's not one you welcome every day; in fact, most of us avoid it.

Welcome the feeling of heartbreak. How was your heart broken? What did it? Who was involved? When did it happen? All of us have memories of heartbreak. Let one or two float into your awareness, and then focus on the one that feels most memorable.

What happened? Watch this scene in your life movie without blame or judgement; just notice what's going on. Why did this have such a big impact on you?

Now ask yourself, "Am I called to do something about this?" If the answer is no, let another memory appear, and another, until you find a memory of heartbreak that connects you with a sense of obligation.

You're searching for your calling in the world. You may already know it. If so, just enjoy these moments of reading and listening to affirm and strengthen your commitment.

Now, create an intention. It might be something like mine: to do whatever I can to help others surrender and win, especially those struggling on the edge of life and death. Your intention, whatever it turns out to be, will always be about helping others. By helping others, you will help yourself.

Don't expect too much right away. Many people don't land on something compelling during the first reading or listening. There's no rush. You can read and listen as often as you want, and daydreaming often teases it out. Rest assured, we all have a calling in this world, and we can find it, when the time is right and if we keep looking. Like fruits on a tree, we all ripen on our own schedule.

When you feel complete or when the audio program is over, write down whatever you want to remember in your journal.

Pause for a few moments before you continue reading. This sort of calm inner experience is what lives at the core of relaxed productivity.

CREATING YOUR HEART COMPASS

We *can* stimulate and experience significant transformation from reading or listening, but it only makes a lasting difference in our lives when we take action afterward. Otherwise, no matter how high the high, it fades into the past to live as a nagging memory that drives us to find the next high. Sounds like an addiction! What makes epiphanies truly valuable is always the disciplined self-regulation in follow-through.

It is essential that you develop the discipline to consistently manage your behaviors, follow through on commitments, and keep your promises.

—JEB BLOUNT

In *Academy of Management Discoveries*, Erik Dane, distinguished associate professor of management at the Jones Graduate School of Business at Rice University, observed, "Epiphanies resolve psychological tension," he says. "It's often something someone has been grappling with that leads to an epiphany. Maybe they're discontent in their career and don't know where to go."

And, recognizing the challenges, he added, "We're often resistant to a solution because it could change our lives or our place within an organization," says Dane. "The real question is, are you psychologically ready for the solution to emerge? If you're not ready for the consequences, you might have mental barricades that hinder problem solving."[26]

> I didn't just hit the wall, have an epiphany, and presto, everything got better. I was compelled to change my lifestyle. I quit chasing all those things "out there" that had been giving me temporary satisfaction and began exploring my inner world, where I often felt like a stranger in a strange land.

---

26   Stephanie Vozza, "This Is How to Have More Epiphanies," Fast Company, May 24, 2019, https://www.fastcompany.com/90353189/this-is-how-to-have-more-epiphanies.

I still find myself chasing things, but I know better now. I listen to my inner voice, and I can actually hear it. We all know that voice; it's the one that calms us down when someone cuts us off in traffic and we start to go ballistic.

"Hey, Gary, calm the heck down!"

That voice is always there; we've just drowned it out with cell phones, TV, work, soccer practice, and what I call our "busynesses." That saying that idle hands do the devil's work may be true enough, but busy hands can also keep us from fully becoming what God made us to be.

There were difficult changes to make. For instance, it was easy (and a real habit for me) to take credit for something rather than doing a good deed anonymously. Also, I rarely gave others in our organization credit instead of automatically claiming the credit for myself. It was new to be quiet in meetings and invite attention rather than demanding it by overtalking and talking over others.

I think ninety-nine times and find nothing. I stop thinking,
swim in silence, and the truth comes to me.

—ALBERT EINSTEIN

People began to notice that I was doing the opposite of what I did before. They started asking me, "What made you do that?" or "What's going on?" They could see that I was changing, that I was letting things happen instead of making them happen. My intuition began to improve, because I was exercising it more often.

I had to learn how to adopt healthy habits like meditation and prayer
to relieve anxiety instead of relying on binge drinking and pills.

In *Blink*, Malcolm Gladwell talks about accessing and trusting our intuition. He writes, "What if we stopped scanning the horizon with our binoculars and began instead examining our own decision making and behavior through the most powerful of microscopes?"[27]

It's our vivid connection with that higher power, I believe, that's prompting our intuition. So, what if we trusted it to help us make decisions? I call this using our "heart compass" because it involves *feeling*, not just *thinking*. The Bible described this higher power expressing itself as a "still, small voice." I couldn't hear mine for decades because my head was so full of noise. I was always multitasking, with a TV on, email up, texts dinging, feeding my addiction to chasing the next deal.

> *In a few seconds or minutes, we realize something*
> *that might influence our lives for decades.*
>
> **—CHIP AND DAN HEATH**

I've learned that when we listen better, we hear more—like a whisper that becomes a wise instruction the moment impatience begins to erupt: "Hey, relax, it's OK. Chill!"

April 21, 2017, is a day I'll never forget.

I'm holed up in a hotel room, wallowing in self-pity. Something beyond embarrassing has just happened that forces me to confront the full disaster of my life. I can't imagine anyone forgiving me now, and forgiving myself seems impossible.

Then the impossible actually happens. It starts with my wife. She forgives me. I can't believe it. I cling to the phone, my

---

27 Malcolm Gladwell, *Blink* (Boston: Little, Brown, 2005), 16.

hand shaking, and the room begins to glow. I can hear Harley-Davidsons rumble in the distance—it's bike week in Myrtle Beach. The sun is setting, and I begin to feel sleepy. I haven't slept without the aid of alcohol for over three years.

The next thing I know it's nine the next morning. I awake in terrible physical pain, but something has changed my heart while I slept. For the first time in many years, I feel optimistic and hopeful about the future.

You see, before I fell asleep, I said three words: "It's over, God." Those three words and forgiveness from my wife created a new beginning. That morning, facing the next chapter in my life, I ask myself, "How can I get better so I can help my family and my friends?"

Getting better meant learning how to be myself and help others. Michelangelo said that he just removed what didn't belong to reveal David, who already lived within the stone he was carving. The true me, complete with the why that centers my life, was already present. Finding and living it became the adventure of my lifetime, because it's what my lifetime is for.

Release the burden. Letting go has all the answers.

—HIRAL NAGDA

The paradox for this chapter—*You can't get here from there*—will mean more to you now. Continuing on this learning path will incrementally turn "nowhere" into "now here."

NEXT:

How the Lifestyle can work for you.

Why Is There Never Enough Time to Do Things Right, But Always Enough Time to Do Them Over?

*Expediency drives us
to take shortcuts,
but kicking the can down the road
doesn't get rid of the can.*

*Eventually, we must be accountable
for the repercussions from our actions.*

Why not just do things right the first time?

CHAPTER SIX

The Success Paradox Lifestyle

And once the storm is over, you won't remember how you made it through, how you managed to survive. You won't even be sure, whether the storm is really over. But one thing is certain. When you come out of the storm, you won't be the same person who walked in. That's what this storm's all about.

—HARUKI MURAKAMI

It's June 2017. I leave rehab and get home just before my son Clemons graduates from high school. Like all dads, I'd hoped to be a hero to my son. All I've been able to do is transfer money into his bank account, praying that it doesn't overdraw my account. My situation is embarrassing for the whole family.

I've lost my swagger, my sea legs, and feel like a man without a country. The crazy part is, this is my "country," my family and my company. But my wife and kids don't trust me, and the partners have met with attorneys to understand their rights if I crash and burn. I can't blame them; I would be doing the same if I wasn't the majority owner. I know it's not entirely personal;

they are justifiably concerned that my behavior is putting our company at risk.

I'm forced to face facts. Not just about myself but about the corporate culture I've created. The company is serving the owners rather than the owners serving the company and our customers. This has to change.

WE WERE HARDLY THE FIRST COMPANY to get things backward. Scores of hugely successful organizations run by executives supposedly much smarter than me have eventually collapsed due to greed and/ or mismanagement. There's a long list, but here are a few familiar names: Enron, Toys "R" Us, Blockbuster, Woolworths, K-Mart, and Lehman Brothers.

> *Earth provides enough to satisfy every man's needs,*
> *but not every man's greed.*
> **—MAHATMA GANDHI**

I was lucky. I escaped both a personal terminal diagnosis and a near miss with our company, thanks to my partners hanging in there long enough for me to get back on track. But facing facts and actually making necessary big changes is hard. Fortunately for us all, I was suffering enough pain, personal and corporate, to make those changes. It was humbling, to say the least.

Some people are born with humility, some never get it, and some acquire it over time. I'm a late bloomer.

When I realized that I was much better in business than I was in my personal life I began running my personal life like a business.

This included beginning to conduct daily check-ins with myself and making sure that I wasn't causing pain to others. I call this "preventative maintenance." I also created a mission, vision, and core values for myself as well as a one-, three-, and five-year goals.

WHY DON'T WE CARE?

Why don't we care enough to do this sort of thing regularly? Why is it so difficult to resist the lure of instant gratification to act intelligently in ways that create a better future for ourselves, our companies, our communities, and our world? The following anecdote introduces a remedy, something called "future thinking."

A king summons the royal gardener to get his advice on planting a certain tree. "Sire," cautions the gardener, "that tree takes over a hundred years to bear fruit."

"Very well," replies the monarch. "You better plant it as soon as possible."

Future thinking means that we care about creating a livable future for our great-great-grandchildren. But we need to think like a king or a queen who cares about those we feel responsible for and accountable to. Here's the problem with this: our very brains conspire against us.

To be a visionary leader, the future must be your home.
—EMMANUEL APETSI

According to recent brain research, "When you think about yourself, a region of the brain known as the medial prefrontal cortex, or MPFC, powers up … The further out in time you try to imagine your own life, the less activation you show in the MPFC. In other words, your brain acts as if your future self is someone you don't know very well and, frankly, someone you don't care about."[28]

This explains why long-range humanitarian sentiments can easily lose out to short-term gratification. Blame the brain! After all, if we imagine that self in the future is not us, why should we care about what happens to him or her?

A few years ago, a prominent White House official made headlines when he scoffed at concerns raised about automation replacing workers. "That's not even on our radar," he boasted, insisting that it wouldn't be an issue for fifty years or more.

Future thinking means that we care about creating a livable future for our great-great-grandchildren.

He was wrong. Almost seven hundred thousand American jobs have already been lost to automation, according to an MIT study. But why didn't he care about the workers who will get replaced in fifty years? He couldn't feel empathy for strangers who didn't really exist, because he wouldn't either … not in that future.

Scores of business books champion putting people first. What's the reality on the ground? I've read accounts of how companies do things for their employees, like improve the lighting. Great. But that's impersonal. What's often missing is the humanity.

"Big company small" remains our internal mantra. This means

---

28   Jane McGonigal, "Our Puny Human Brains Are Terrible at Thinking about the Future," Slate, April 13, 2017, https://slate.com/technology/2017/04/why-people-are-so-bad-at-thinking-about-the-future.html.

that we care about our staff and our customers, not just to improve productivity but because this is what human beings do. Caring for each other is obviously an incredible investment in the future, because adults raise children, then their children grow up to have jobs and children themselves. The positive ripple effect echoing into the future from being personable with each other in the workplace is impossible to fully calculate.

What helps develop our future-thinking skills is to simplify. In *Traction*, Gino Wickman wrote: "I used to worry about 100 different things. Once I learned there were six components to my business and I focused on only those, those 100 different things I'd been worrying about went away."[29]

Well, we only have three: being authentic, doing good, and doing well. These are the three principles of the SPL, a formula that helps deal with that brain problem.

Simplicity is ultimately a matter of focus.

—ANN VOSKAMP

THE SUCCESS PARADOX LIFESTYLE

The SPL is based on those three principles. Each has a primary emotion and an activating emotion, a core concept, and a practice for integration. Here's the quick overview. You'll be able to dive deeper as we go along and, in Part Three, craft your own strategic plan for living this way.

---

29 Gino Wickman, *Traction*, (Dallas: BenBella Books, 2011), 3.

PRINCIPLE	EMOTION	ACTIVATOR	CORE CONCEPT	PRACTICE
Being Authentic	Gratitude	Humility	The more we become dependent on a higher power, the more independent we are.	Daily self-examination
Doing Good	Compassion	Grief	We are all born to care. Environments support or suppress that capacity.	Servant leadership
Doing Well	Generosity	Love	Generate profit by doing good and share the wealth.	Full profit economics

PRINCIPLE ONE: BEING AUTHENTIC

The key to being authentic is to surrender to a higher power, however conceived. We admit that we cannot manage our lives on our own. We surrender and lose that responsibility, but we simultaneously surrender and win by gaining the greatest ally imaginable.

What activates letting go is humility. It usually takes a big whack on the side of the head to jolt us out of the arrogance that drives our micromanaging. In surrender, we discover another paradox: the more dependent we become on a higher power, the more independent we actually are. It's like depending on a car so we can travel independently on the road.

True humility is not thinking less of yourself;
it is thinking of yourself less.

—RICK WARREN

Our recommended practice is a time-out in the morning and a review at day's end, plus a midday check-in. These are special moments reserved for being, not doing,

The key to being authentic is to surrender to a higher power.

intended to make our relationship with that higher power an experience, not just a theory.

PRINCIPLE TWO: DOING GOOD

Demi Lovato is a superstar who has been transparent about her addiction issues. She wrote, "I'm a firm believer in leaving this world a better place for future generations. Being a public figure has presented me with so many extraordinary opportunities to give back, to volunteer, and to touch so many lives along the way. I've had the privilege of advocating for children and adults all over the world dealing with bullying, eating disorders, and mental health issues. Everyone has causes close to their hearts, so whatever you're passionate about, do something to make a difference."[30]

---

30   Demi Lovato, *Stay Strong* (Chicago: R.R. Donnelley, 2011), July 27 entry.

> Doing good is about helping others. All of us are born to care, it's in our nature as human beings. The environments we live in—early family experiences, office environments, etc.—either support or suppress that capacity.

What activates compassion is connecting with our own suffering. This usually happens through grief, an emotion we traditionally suppress in this culture. What really helps is an encounter with mortality, our own or another. More on that in a moment.

Compassion, or empathy, is fundamentally different than sympathy, which enables others to identify as victims. The practice we recommend is community service, especially to help those you've judged to be less than you.

PRINCIPLE THREE: DOING WELL

Some economic experts say that we need to invent a better financial system. Probably. But why not model it after what works and has always worked, no matter what "the market" does? It's staring us in the face: nature.

Nature operates on the principle of reciprocal generosity. For instance, as Beronda L. Montgomery from Michigan State University wrote, "Mycorrhizal connections can link multiple plants in a functioning network. When plants produce more sugars than they need, they can share them via this interconnected root fungal network. By doing so, they ensure that all plants in the community have access to the energy they need to support their growth."[31]

We've created a society that values hoarding over balance.

Imagine one part of your body keeping all the blood. That would make the whole body sick. We stay healthy because the trillions of cells, the organs, all the systems in our bodies cooperate together.

I am happy because I want nothing from anyone.

—ALBERT EINSTEIN

Generosity is our core emotion, activated by love for life, love for our families and friends, and love for our work and for the planet. It is our home, after all.

Our practice is what we call "full-profit economics," generating wealth for all to enjoy.

---

31   Nicola J Day, "How Plants Talk to Each Other and Learn to Share," The Conversation, April 24, 2021, *https://www.inverse.com/science/plants-talk-to-each-other#:~:text=Mycorrhizal%20connections%20can%20link%20multiple,need%20to%20support%20their%20growth.*

MORE ON FUTURE THINKING

We quoted from Jane McGonigal at the beginning of this chapter. She's a research director at the Institute for the Future, a nonprofit based in Palo Alto, California. Running a survey on future thinking, they discovered that one particular event seems to stimulate the brain to think more about the future:

> A brush with mortality, such as a potentially terminal medical diagnosis, a near-death experience, or other traumatic event.

> Brushes with mortality are often associated, in the psychological literature with a renewed effort to lead a meaningful life and leave a positive legacy behind. Thinking about, planning for, and contributing to our shared long-term futures may be an essential part of laying the groundwork for both.[32]

> *Isn't it sad that so often it takes facing death*
> *to appreciate life and each other fully?*
> **—LORI EARL**

I sure had my brush with mortality, when a doctor informed me that I probably had less than a month to live. My writing partner, Will, survived near-lethal food poisoning and an unfriendly encounter with his chainsaw. Nothing gets our attention and motivates big changes like facing death, our own or that of someone near and dear to us.

In Frank Capra's classic film, *It's A Wonderful Life*, the protagonist, George Bailey, comes to his own life-and-death moment. His suicide attempt is thwarted by an angel who tricks George into saving him (by doing good). Threatened by a financial emergency in his town,

---

32   McGonigal, "Our Puny Human Brains."

which George blames on himself, he declares, "I wish I'd never been born!" The angel takes George into a future where he doesn't exist, a world where he *never* existed. He witnesses firsthand the devastating impact of his absence, comes to his senses, and begs, "Please, God, let me live again." He returns to the present (now being his authentic self) to discover that the generosity of his neighbors has saved their town, so it can prosper again (doing well).

Not all of us have faced a personal encounter with death. But we all know someone who has died, so we've all had to deal with this ultimate loss. Grief is virtually taboo in our culture, so it's likely we're carrying around a measure of unfelt sorrow.

Journaling on the three instructions that follow will help you tap into that reservoir by simulating a "brush with mortality." Visit successparadoxbook.com for an audio simulation.

CONFRONTING MORTALITY

Describe how you feel about a near-death experience you've had and/or your reaction to the death of someone you loved.

_____

_____

_____

_____

Take a few moments to close your eyes and relive the experience. Give yourself permission to feel more now than you did then. Journal what happens.

_____

_____

_____

_____

Imagine receiving a terminal diagnosis. Faced with a limited number of days left, how would you change your lifestyle?

_____

_____

_____

_____

MORNING TIME-OUT

Hopefully, you've been experimenting with this since we introduced it in chapter one. This simple practice helps you focus on "being," before you plunge into a day full of "doing."

Meditate or pray, with no intention at all. Read from one of the many daily message books out there. We recommend Demi Lovato's book, *Stay Strong*. How long should your morning time-out be? It depends on your schedule and your preferences. Fifteen to thirty minutes is a good range.

NOON CHECK-IN

Set a phone alert for noon every day. When the chime sounds, pause for a moment of reflection. How are you doing so far today? Are there any course corrections you might want to make? Remember, you can start your day over as many times as you need or want to. You can make a bad day good with a new choice.

DAY'S END REVIEW

This practice is about reviewing what happened during the day, to celebrate wins and learning. Taking time like this helps you complete unfinished business. It also keeps your life uncluttered with nagging memories, so you can focus on your present-moment experience.

THE LIFESTYLE SCORESHEET

I love business because we measure our results. I already mentioned that when I realized I was better in business than life, I began to manage my life like a business. But how do we measure our life results?

We created this ten-question scoresheet to calculate our success with the Lifestyle. It only takes a few minutes, and we've provided space for recording your score now and later, as you repeat the exercise to track your progress over time. You can fill this out here or access the form on our website, successparadoxbook.com.

For each statement below, check the appropriate box from 1 to 5: 1 for strongly no, 5 for absolutely yes, 2–4 for degrees in between. Trust your first intuitive answer.

	1	2	3	4	5
You proactively face difficult facts about your personal life and career.					
You are skilled at "future thinking," able to strategize toward optimizing long-term results.					
You are a humble person, which your friends would confirm.					
You frequently feel grateful.					
You care about others and prioritize helping them.					
When you see others suffering, you feel genuine sadness.					

	1	2	3	4	5
You love your life and your work.					
You are eager to create profit and share it.					
You have journaled, above, and / or listened to the audio program in this chapter. No (zero points) Yes (5 points).					
You are doing the morning, noon, and evening time-out and review sessions regularly.					

Total your scores and multiply by two. This is your percentage score. Redoing this questionnaire periodically will help you track your progress.

DATE: _____   SCORE: _____

DATE: _____   SCORE: _____

DATE: _____   SCORE: _____

DATE: _____   SCORE: _____

The paradox for this chapter is about expediency versus future thinking. When we master the three principles of the SPL and fully embody them, we create and sustain a positive ripple effect in our personal lives and in the world at large.

As the saying goes, "Touch a flower, disturb a star."

NEXT:

The power of giving up.

Give to Receive, Receive to Give

To have more, we need to get more, right?

Only when we limit our wealth to personal possessions.

Nature operates on the principle of shared wealth.

*Likewise, we can live interdependently,
connected to each other and all other life forms.*

*Giving and receiving are mutually profitable activities
that sustain balance and health.*

CHAPTER SEVEN

Giving Up

*I want to give up my bearings, slip out of who I am,
shed everything, the way a snake discards old skin.*

—KHALED HOSSEINI

*We've just sold a business, and the final numbers are coming in.
One of the owners, a woman who'd worked hard building the
organization for years, is hoping to walk away with 2 million.
When she learns it will only be 1.5, she's disappointed but takes
it in good spirits.*

*I don't. I know she deserves more. I petition several of my siblings
who are minor owners. They agree, and we chip in the five
hundred thousand.*

*I remember the look on this woman's face as I hand her the
check. You cherish moments like that forever.*

*Years later, out of the blue, she calls me. "Gary," she says, her
voice urgent, "there's a great business you could buy, but you*

gotta move fast." I do. The business I buy because of her tip becomes my most successful venture ever.

GENEROSITY INSPIRES GENEROSITY. But it only works when there are no strings attached. And sometimes it's not easy to track the connection between something given and something received. My writing partner told me about one of his first jobs, working as a mail man in Alberta, where he grew up. That winter it

> Generosity inspires generosity. But it only works when there are no strings attached.

dropped to thirty below and stayed there for a month. The Canadian post office didn't use jeeps in those days, so he trudged through snow every day.

So did the elderly man working the route next to him, and Will worried that this old guy might collapse in a snowbank and freeze to death. So they cut a deal. Will delivered the last thirty minutes of this guy's morning mail and then met him at a coffee shop, where this grateful gentleman treated them to coffee, pie, and fascinating conversations. Will didn't get paid more for doing more work, but he still fondly remembers their exchange. His old friend lived to retire the next year.

Our separation from each other is an optical illusion.

—ALBERT EINSTEIN

In chapter one we advocated for turning our lives over to a higher power. We made that appealing by listing mind-blowing statistics that described what that universal intelligence is managing, like beating our hearts and steering the stars.

And … giving us this gift of life. What's that worth? It's priceless, obviously. We could give every day for the rest of our lives and never repay that debt. Fortunately, no one is keeping track!

When we give generously, we're working off that debt.

You give your all, and yet you always feel as if it costs you nothing.

—SIMONE DE BEAUVOIR

GIVING UP AND BEING ACCOUNTABLE

It's another special day, the day I fire myself.

Our health care company hadn't been growing fast enough for my taste. Being the "boss," I tried to speed things up. But my impulsive strategy blew up, and two key managers resigned. Fallout quickly spread throughout the company.

We hold a meeting with all the injured parties present. Sharon, our coach, launches an exercise: "What were the biggest mistakes you've ever made?" When it's my turn, I feel every eye in the room burning into me. I look around the room, mention this misguided initiative, and confess: "I was an asshole." I'll never forget the reactions. Shock, confusion, curiosity. "What the hell happened to Gary?"

"I thought I was invincible," I continue. "I thought I knew it all." I make eye contact with Andra, who is a registered pharmacist, and Brandi, who is a registered nurse as well. "I had no respect for your licenses. I'm not a nurse or a pharmacist. I had no qualifications. I should never have done what I did, and I

will never do anything like that again. In fact, I'm removing myself from any form of management so you will never, ever have to deal with the possibility of me doing that again."

I'll never forget Andra's sudden smile and then her tears. Nothing I could say would ever take away the pain I'd caused her and others, but I know she is grateful for my apology. Her feelings are finally being validated. It's a miracle moment for us both, and our relationship has since blossomed, not to mention what's happened with other key players in our company.

They understand that I have voluntarily stepped down, and they will never be under my impulsive influence again. The healing in that room feels like the healing in my hotel room the day I quit drinking. The medicine? Forgiveness.

They are inspired to work with David to make us the most successful company of our kind in the country.

THE DRAMA TRIANGLE

Here's something else to give up on, drama in relationships! I sure had my share and wish I'd known about this model I'm about to introduce back when I was in my wrestling match with life.

Stephen Karpman, MD, was a young American psychiatrist when he "observed that in conflict and drama, there is 'good guy vs bad guy' thinking. He also observed that the participants become drawn in, even seduced, by the energy that the drama generates. The drama obscures the real issues. Confusion and upset escalates. Solutions are no longer the focus."

He created what's become known as *The Drama Triangle*. "Karpman defined three roles in the 'transaction': Persecutor, Rescuer (the one up positions) and Victim (one down position). Karpman placed these three roles on an inverted triangle and described them as being the three aspects, or faces of drama."[33]

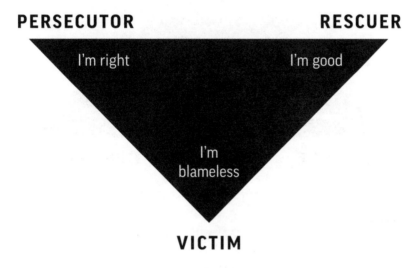

PERSECUTOR
I'm right

RESCUER
I'm good

I'm blameless

VICTIM

No one is ever a victim, although your conquerors would have you believe in your own victimhood. How else could they conquer you?

—BARBARA MARCINIAK

When things go south, it's typical to identify as a victim, blame someone else, and hope to get rescued. The persecutor could be the boss, a spouse, another company, the falling stock market, etc. The rescuer takes many forms. My favorite was alcohol. And work.

---

33   R. Skip Johnson, "Escaping Conflict and the Karpman Drama Triangle," BPD Family, January 4, 2021, https://www.bpdfamily.com/content/karpman-drama-triangle.

*Giving up on the drama triangle means
turning everything upside down.*

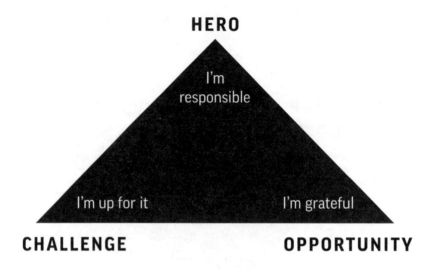

Here are the three steps for pulling off a sweet 180:

1. Change identities from being a victim to the hero of your own life story.

2. Turn the bad guy or wrong situation into a welcome challenge.

3. Forget being rescued; embrace an opportunity for service and personal growth.

I can remember being seriously trapped in this drama triangle and how exhausting it was to try fixing things without changing positions. I had to quit being the victim or the rescuer (my preferred role). Knowing that I could choose to be the hero of my own life story would have helped me back then!

But I also would have needed education about that myth of self-sufficiency. So many of us men suffer from the John Wayne Syndrome, as I call it. This quote—which seems cool at first—actually exposes the problem we're addressing:

> *"You can't just wait for someone to give you what you want. You've got to make it happen for yourself."*

Sure, we need to be responsible for ourselves. But this sentiment emphasizes "every man for himself." Imagine that comment altered to champion the Success Paradox:

> *"We're surrounded by people who can help us live our best life. And we can help them."*

My ego is doing push-ups every day, getting stronger and poised to take credit for the great things that happen and blame someone else for the goofs. I have to counter that with everything I can to increase my authenticity. Number-one strategy? Humility. I'm a work in progress—we all are—and nothing reveals that more than how we are in relationships.

Einstein defined insanity as doing the same thing and expecting different results. Giving up on the drama triangle is doing something different. We've defined giving up in two ways, and both work. Maybe it's right to walk away like I did in that meeting. Maybe it's appropriate to be generous, the way my partners and I rewarded a loyal colleague. Referencing these two definitions, use this worksheet below to begin analyzing the patterns in your life. Start with one item; you can think of others later.

THE GIVING UP WORKSHEET

Fill out this worksheet here or visit successparadoxbook.com.

Describe one situation where you need to give up to achieve a different result.

_____

_____

_____

_____

What are you holding on to—identity or behaviors—that contributes to that result?

_____

_____

_____

_____

On a scale of 1–10, how willing are you to give up and change what you are doing?

_____ of 10

What could motivate you to become even more willing to give up?

_____

_____

_____

_____

What are a few changes you might make immediately?

_____

_____

_____

_____

EVEN GOD RESTED ON THE SEVENTH DAY

We recovering workaholics/do-aholics are in a very large club! Justin Blanton was a workaholic attorney in California. He reported to WebMD: "Whether I'm reading a Harry Potter book on my PDA while waiting in the deli line, checking email on my phone as soon as my date makes for the ladies room, or heading back to my computer each commercial break (no TiVo ... yet)—I'm always checking something."[34]

Justin illuminates one of the most difficult things to give up: the habit (obsession) of managing our lives with conscious attention. It's more than a belief; it's a personal operating system. It's also a disease millions of teenagers have caught from their addiction to social media. We cover that in the next chapter.

What we put our attention on matters.

Attention doesn't hold our world together. When we believe it does, even unconsciously (and it's almost always unconscious), we simply can't allow ourselves to rest, because we're afraid everything would fall apart.

Relax, recharge and reflect. Sometimes it's OK to do nothing.

—IZEY VICTORIA ODIASE

---

34   Neil Osterweil, "Are You a Workaholic?," WebMD, January 29, 2020, https://www.webmd.com/balance/features/are-you-a-workaholic.

A man stands by his open window all night, using a bucket to scoop through the air. Sunrise arrives, and he collapses to the floor, exhausted but relieved.

"I did it!" he proclaims proudly. "I finally got all the darkness out of this room."

That guy was me. I never rested. I swear that I worked in my sleep. There was always another phone call to make, emails to answer, texts to send, and meetings to schedule (then miss because I was over-scheduled). If Guinness had a category for do-aholics, I'd be listed in there as the world champion! All this changed when a friend showed me a simple diagram that explains the power of rest.

REST   **WORK**

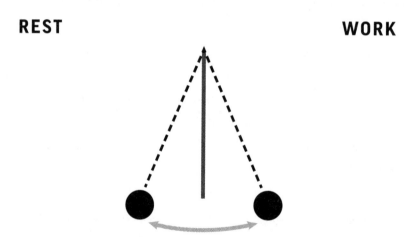

Imagine a pendulum swinging from rest to work and back again. At first glance, you might observe, "But I'm never resting, and I'm always working, so this pendulum idea can't apply to me." It does. Let's add some clarifying detail to explain how.

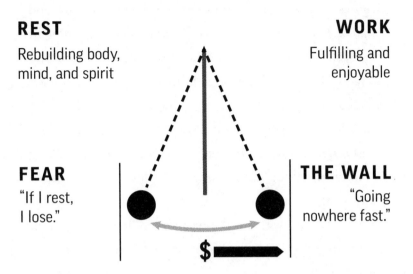

REST
Rebuilding body,
mind, and spirit

WORK
Fulfilling and
enjoyable

FEAR
"If I rest,
I lose."

THE WALL
"Going
nowhere fast."

Our inability or refusal to rest creates a wall to success. We can push all we want, but work won't be fulfilling or enjoyable, even if we hit our financial goals. Now let's see what happens when we give up our obsession with work and begin to value rest.

REST

WORK

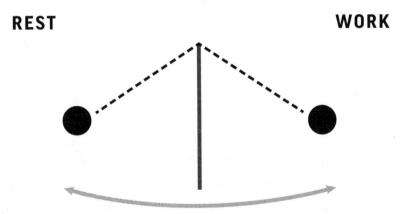

Momentum builds in both directions. Embracing rest sends us into work with more energy. Relaxing from work lets us rest more deeply.

Figures as different as Charles Dickens, Henri Poincaré, and Ingmar Bergman, working in disparate fields in different times, all shared a passion for their work, a terrific ambition to succeed, and an almost superhuman capacity to focus. Yet when you look closely at their daily lives, they only spent a few hours a day doing what we would recognize as their most important work. The rest of the time, they were hiking mountains, taking naps, going on walks with friends, or just sitting and thinking. Their creativity and productivity, in other words, were not the result of endless hours of toil. Their towering creative achievements result from modest "working" hours.

How did they manage to be so accomplished? Can a generation raised to believe that 80-hour workweeks are necessary for success learn something from the lives of the people who directed *Wild Strawberries*, laid the foundations of chaos theory and topology, and wrote *Great Expectations*?[35]

> *A flawless delusion is more appealing to the*
> *human mind than a flawed reality.*
> **—ABHIJIT NASKAR**

Maria Shriver uses this quote on her blog, *Deliberate Rest: Why the Secret to Success Is Taking a Break*. She concluded: "If you recognize that work and rest are two sides of the same coin, that you can get more from rest by getting better at it and that by giving it a place in

---

35 Alex Soojung-Kim Pang, "Darwin Was a Slacker and You Should Be Too," Nautilus, March 28, 2017, https://nautil.us/darwin-was-a-slacker-and-you-should-be-too-236532/.

your life you'll stand a better chance of living the life you want, you'll be able to do your job, and your life's work, better."[36]

Hey, how about a family break? I'm mentioning my kids a few times during the book, hoping not to embarrass them too much! It seems like a good time to say a few words about Sutton, our youngest.

He's a natural-born organizer. When he was just four and we were heading out on a holiday, he asked me—he had this crazy deep voice—"How many days are we going, Daddy?" I said "Five." He packed five days of warm-weather clothes, but on day three he looked at me, serious as a judge, and asked: "Does I has to wear day three underwear?"

He and I seem to share the same wavelength, maybe because we're both the fourth child in our families. He's always been a planner, a keen observer, and a leader. Pretty damn funny too, as you can tell. He was ten when I was turning my big corner, and I remember him asking me about work. I'd just shifted from working out of town almost all of the time to restricting my away time and working out of the house three days and nights every week. He asked when I'd be hitting the road again, and I told him I was home for good.

"I like that," he said. "Life is good now, having you around." That was so gratifying to hear.

THE OBSERVER EFFECT

Learning how to rest and appreciating how rest contributed to my success at work forced me to question my habits, my beliefs, and the way I managed my day-to-day life. But I learned there was something even more radical involved, the influence of perception itself.

---

36 Maria Shriver, "Deliberate Rest: Why the Secret to Success Is Taking a Break," Maria Shriver, accessed October 2, 2022, https://mariashriver.com/sharon-salzberg-affection-well-being-2/.

Scientists understand something that most of us don't: the act of looking changes what we're looking at. In physics, researchers try to manage this problem by minimizing the influence exerted by their instruments of observation. For instance, to see something requires light. But light distorts what's being observed. So they experiment with using as little light as possible for as brief a time as possible, to try and see something behaving almost the way it does when they're not looking.

The way we look changes what we see.

That popular phrase skeptics use, "I'll believe it when I see it," is more accurately stated as "I'll see it when I believe it." This acknowledges the influence of bias. For instance, if we believe an employee is lazy, we will tend to find proof to confirm that. If a colleague is an old school buddy, we will tend to *not* see behaviors that contradict our belief that he is a fine person.

When we believe that our success depends on conscious attention anchored to constant work, we *will* gather proof to strengthen *that* belief. We might "see" others progressing faster than we are in their careers (because they're working even harder than we are). If we believe that resting is laziness, we can prove that too. But we're cherry-picking evidence, seeing what we believe.

> *Whatever good or bad fortune may come our way we can always give it meaning and transform it into something of value.*
>
> **—HERMANN HESSE**

Blogging about his book, *Why You Get More Done When You Work Less,* Alex Soojung-Kim Pang makes a suggestion: "Think of rest as akin to sex or singing or running. Everyone basically knows how to do it, but with a little work and understanding, you can learn to do it a lot better."[37]

Rest has become a thing in my life, and I'm amazed how much more productive I am doing less work in less time but accomplishing more, with space to enjoy my family and leisure hours without judging myself for being lazy. The tangible results in my business prove this *is* a best practice. I give myself the gift of rest and I receive the reward of improved productivity.

Rest has become a thing in my life, and I'm amazed how much more productive I am.

"Give to receive, receive to give." That's the primary paradox we're exploring here. The simplest metaphor is breathing. During an asthma attack, it becomes difficult to breathe out, so air gets trapped in the lungs, which means there's no room to breathe in new air. That's what happens when we're reluctant to give. There's less room to receive. Likewise, when we struggle to receive, we have less to give.

THE GIVING UP SCORECARD

You can fill this out here or access it through our website, success-paradoxbook.com.

For each statement below, check the appropriate box from 1 to 5: 1 for strongly no, 5 for absolutely yes, 2–4 for degrees in between. Trust your first intuitive answer.

---

37   Alex Soojung-Kim Pang, "Why You Get More Done When You Work Less," *Greater Good Magazine*, May 11, 2017, https://greatergood.berkeley.edu/article/item/how_resting_more_can_boost_your_productivity.

	1	2	3	4	5
I understand the meaning and value of giving up, as explained, and I am doing it.					
My new bottom line starts with being authentic.					
I understand the Drama Triangle and am consciously avoiding all three roles.					
I agree with Einstein's definition of insanity (doing the same thing but expecting a different result), so I am changing what I do (and how I think).					
I realize how important rest is for remaining productive and healthy.					
I rest every day.					
I know that the Observer Effect is operative in every moment of my life, so I am becoming more vigilant about how I choose to see people and situations.					
I understand and agree with the term: "I will see it when I believe it."					
I have made a one-year commitment to learn and live the SPL.					
I will use the tracking system (below).					

Total each column, add together, and multiply by two to determine your percent score.

SCORING RESULTS (%)

0-25   Giving up is difficult for you. Pick one situation to experiment with and grow from one success.

26-50   You realize that giving up is not weakness; it's about being honest. Use the Lifestyle Tracker every day (below).

51-75   Giving up is becoming a daily habit. Notice when you do and when you hang on and how each feels.

76-100   Giving up is a solid part of your daily lifestyle. Explore using the Giving Up audio program to deepen your inner experience.

Visit successparadoxbook.com for access.

DATE: _____ SCORE: _____

THE LIFESTYLE TRACKING SYSTEM

You can fill this out here or access on our website, successparadox-book.com.

Our Lifestyle Tracking System measures progress day by day, weekly, and monthly. We've reproduced it here for easy photocopying, and it's also accessible via our website, successparadoxbook.com, where you can download and print.

Check boxes where you can honestly say, "Yes, I did that!"

LIFESTYLE TRACKER FOR WEEK OF _____

		MON	TUES	WED	THURS	FRI	TOTAL
I WAS AUTHENTIC							
1	At work						
	In life						
	Relationships						
	With myself						
	TOTALS						
I DID GOOD							
2	At work						
	With family and friends						
	With strangers						
	In my community						
	For the larger world						
	TOTALS						
I DID WELL *(at work)*							
3	Increased value						
	Was generous						
	Good in meetings						
	Sensible management						
	Experienced growth						
	TOTALS						
ONE-WEEK TOTAL							

Add up the three totals to get your grand total for
Authenticity ___, Doing Good ___, and Doing Well ___.

MONTHLY TOTALS FOR MONTH OF _____

Add up and enter the weekly totals for each month.

MONTH	BEING AUTHENTIC	DOING GOOD	DOING WELL	TOTALS
January				
February				
March				
April				
May				
June				
July				
August				
September				
October				
November				
December				
TOTAL				

These forms enable you to track your progress and identify where you are flourishing and where you may be stuck.

NEXT:

What does it take to make big changes?

We Can Get What We Need When We Quit Trying to Get What We Want

Pushing for what we want

often blinds us from seeing

that we already have what we need.

Being grateful for what is

restores our vision.

CHAPTER EIGHT

Opening to Big Change

When people can think and lead with heart, then I turn my head. Big lovers are more than just passionate. They also have the ability to turn down the noise and reflect in order to generate the best and wisest solutions.

This sometimes quieter leadership is about being genuine, caring, and true to one's goals and values.

The primary role of leaders is not to wow with winning ideas, but to make sure the organization lives up to its principles and dreams.

—HOWARD BEHAR, STARBUCKS

WE SLEEP ABOUT A THIRD OF OUR LIVES, 230,000 hours during an average lifetime, yet most of us pay more attention and invest much more money in our cars than our beds. Why? In part, because no one but our spouse and kids sees the bed, and we care more about what people see us driving around in.

Likewise, another third of our lives is spent at work, about ninety thousand hours on average before retirement (although this pattern is changing dramatically with remote working agreements).

So why don't we invest more in the working environments of our organizations?

Dennis Bakke comments: "Why do so many people work so hard so they can escape to Disneyland? Why are video games more popular than work? … Why do many workers spend years dreaming about and planning for retirement? The reason is simple and dispiriting. We have made the workplace a frustrating and joyless place where people do what they're told and have few ways to participate in decisions or fully use their talents."[38]

Likewise, another third of our lives is spent at work, about ninety thousand hours on average before retirement.

People don't care about the workplace environment for the same reason they don't spend more money on a bed.
They don't understand how important it is.

Fortunately for our organization, we learned about this in time to make major changes before the dysfunctional elements woven deeply into our company culture could sabotage us. Big change had to start at the top.

The bottom line is determined by those at the top.

—LJUPKA CVETANOVA

---

38   Chris Munshar, untitled blog, Medium.com, November 6, 2019, https://medium.com/@Chrismunshaw/why-do-so-many-people-work-so-hard-so-they-can-escape-to-disneyland-27608a7095dc.

F.O.G.

We had many leaders in our organization who had assumed their positions over time for one reason or another. Plus, we were bumping up against one hundred employees, and that's a tough hurdle to clear unless you identify and eliminate what's in the way. Our problem was easy to find: F.O.G. This stood for "Friend of Gary." The company was full of my friends. I'd created a culture where people were hired, promoted, and even given raises based on the status of their relationship with me rather than their skills or merit.

> I had to get out of the way. This is a hard thing for any founder or entrepreneur to do. I'd already fired myself and appointed David as the new CEO. But it was another big step to empower him to radically change our organizational culture by getting rid of the F.O.G. factor.

Some longtime employees had to go. Imagine what that was like for me. I felt like I was turning my back on friends. But I had to separate friendship from work. Coach Sharon assured me that this would actually help my personal life blossom while improving our business culture. Time proved she was right, but that didn't make the "purge," as I thought of it, any easier.

As David and Sharon guided a real cleanup operation for Palmetto, I looked back and realized that because I hadn't done this before, I'd actually sold six other companies prematurely to publicly traded companies or PE firms. If only …

There was a big bonus that arose from this process: liberation for our hardest workers. As holdouts from the old regime left, we could see how our culture had been riddled with gossip and drama. There had been a certain comforting intoxication to that, but it sure didn't lead to productivity or job satisfaction. That problem left with the friends who didn't belong, and it felt like we were pumping oxygen into the room.

Our former president of HR, Sharon, and David established a termination decision-making process and began conducting interviews for new hires. I wasn't included in that process. This clearly demonstrated the end of the F.O.G. era at Palmetto and ensured that we brought in talented folks with the right background and skills. I watched this unfolding and learned how to "say what you mean, without saying it mean." This helped me stop running from conflict, face hard truths, and deal with my mistakes in less stressful and more effective ways.

People are more interested in hiring candidates who acknowledge legitimate weaknesses as opposed to bragging or humblebragging.

—ADAM GRANT

Something truly magnificent began to happen. Our greatest and brightest began bringing us ideas they'd been sitting on for years, like cost-saving tactics and clever customer-service improvements. Creativity began to flourish, and the enthusiasm was contagious. We even created a new employee title: the Boomerang. This described former employees who loved how we helped our patients but had left when we lost our way. They began returning when they learned we were back on track. We regained the appeal of a big company that felt small.

Culture does not make people. People make culture.

—CHIMAMANDA NGOZI ADICHIE

David assembled his senior leadership team. We instituted the incentive practice I'd always used—creating equity ownership for the main contributors. Shares were allotted based on individual contribution rather than being a F.O.G. or happening to be in the right place at the right time. David selected them and chose the numbers, not me. Why not? David had created the budget.

Opening to big change requires facing facts and making tough choices.

As Ryan Holiday, author of *Courage Is Calling*, writes, "It's not the choices that are hard. In fact, the right thing is often obvious. It's the *consequences* and the *costs* of that choice that are hard. It's the complicated, difficult, unpleasant stuff that we adults end up having to wrestle with on the other side of our decisions that make the decisions seem so difficult."[39]

THE PALMETTO EVOLUTION

Here's a quick tour through our history. You will find a more detailed accounting in chapter twelve. We bought Palmetto Infusion in 1998 for $159,000. The company had a single location in Columbia, South Carolina, with fifteen employees and annual revenue of $2 million. Our field was home health care and our goal was to keep patients out of the hospital, so this was a perfect fit for us.

We blew through our line of credit in a month, and my Dad freaked out. We were essentially helping to invent the ambulatory infusion business, which meant that Blue Cross and the other insurers didn't have a payment system in place for us. So, we incurred big bills with no money coming in. We had to trust there was a light at the end of this tunnel, and that it wasn't a train rushing toward us!

---

39   Ryan Holiday, "Welcome to Life. There Are Only Hard Facts and Harder Decisions," RyanHoliday.net, accessed August 4, 2022, https://ryanholiday.net/hard-facts/.

Trust is the foundation on which the business
relationships you build rest.

—JEB BLOUNT

We weathered that storm and by 2007 had grown Palmetto to twelve locations with annual revenue of $40 million. The partners decided to sell, and we did. This afforded an insight into a familiar but paradoxical phenomenon in business. Sometimes partners work together better when they are struggling than when they are making big money!

The new owners also struggled, and we bought Palmetto back in 2011 for $1.2 million. By 2017 we grew annual revenue from $35 to 80 million and replaced annual losses of $1.5 million with profits of $8.5 million. Early on, we learned why the prior owners had failed.

They had only offered drugs they made a sizable profit on, or they would send patients to the hospital. This practice soured their relationship with doctors, and many stopped referring their patients. My first task was to reach out to those doctors and assure them that our approach was the opposite. Send us everyone, I told them, and we'll make sure they are well taken care of, even those who couldn't pay. Our commitment was to help our patients get the lowest prices for the best medicine and to stay out of the hospital, if at all possible.

This was a philosophy that began with my Dad. He always accepted every patient, regardless of their ability to pay. And he was classically entrepreneurial, always seeking new opportunities to provide what his customers, the patients, needed—like access to new and effective drugs at reasonable prices.

Today (2023), Palmetto is flying high, with over five hundred employees, about eleven thousand patients, operating out of forty centers in six states with a valuation just south of $400 million and a compound annual growth rate of 35 percent plus.

> Why did we succeed when the prior owners failed? Because we prioritized doing good before doing well.

The turnaround we orchestrated demonstrates the power of this formula. From many other similar wins, we now fully trust that we will do well by doing good first, because that's the way it's supposed to work. We embrace this as one of our best business practices.

The problem with drama is that it always costs money.

—KEITH J. CUNNINGHAM

It's an emergency. One of our departments suffers a catastrophic failure that creates an estimated $50 to $100 million hit, potentially costing me personally in the neighborhood of $20 million.

The key players meet. I listen. "Money is temporary," I tell them. "Let's work together to find a long-term solution and not worry about the short-term issues."

The room goes quiet. It's not the reaction they were expecting. But I understand that I'm only doing my job when I think and lead with heart. I know how important emotion is to everything we do, especially how we handle emergencies. When I first walked in, there was a tangible feeling of fear in the air, but within minutes we have shifted into gratitude.

They already know how to manage this emergency. All they need from me is to know that doing the right thing will be supported from the top, regardless of the money. That's the formula I/we live by, and it works, in this situation and in every other. We prioritize doing good over profits. We never compromise our values because of fear of loss.

"It's just money," I tell them, quoting Sam Walton, who said that on the day he lost $100 million.

In *Reinventing Organizations*, Frederic Laloux writes, "What is the mood that would best serve the organization at this moment in time so as to achieve its purpose? It might well be playfulness or concentration, but perhaps it is something else altogether—a mood of prudence, joy, pride, care, gratitude, wonder, curiosity, or determination."

Our purpose is to serve our customers, not to make or save money.

Getting in touch with the core emotions attached to our purpose helped us remember this. Fear subsided, gratitude returned, and we began to act from a position of prosperity, not lack. Desperation was replaced by curiosity and creativity. Things worked out fine.

Laloux continued: "Gratitude is a powerful emotion. We declare that we are satisfied. We can drop our search for more; in this moment, we have everything we need. Out of that fullness, other emotions naturally bubble up. We tend to get in touch with joy and generosity, and we treat others with love and care."[40]

He who has a why to live for can bear almost any how.

—FRIEDRICH NIETZSCHE

---

40   Frederic Laloux, *Reinventing Organizations* (Brussels: Nelson Parker, 2014), 218.

A business blogger dug into the issue this way: "It's notoriously difficult for organizations to keep faith with two equally important goals. A lot try. For-profit companies make grand pronouncements about social responsibility, but their resolve nearly always weakens when shareholder earnings are threatened. 'Social' businesses and non-profits often go in the opposite direction, privileging mission over financial viability."[41]

Here's the real problem he's exposing: Having "two equally important goals" is a recipe for conflict. We don't prioritize either social responsibility or shareholder earnings (doing good and doing well in our language). First up for us is personal authenticity. With this firmly in place, not just for me but throughout the company, we handle emergencies from a different perspective.

Who we are being guides us to do good and to do well.

Our experience is that when number one stays number one, two and three fall into place. Personal authenticity requires letting go, which enables a superpower to handle emergencies. Our role is to determine and execute the hopefully wise actions that arise from that guidance, which originates beyond our personal skills and beliefs. We depend on that supernatural intelligence, and we've never been disappointed. BTW, I'd suggest that a debate about this is irrelevant unless those involved have actually experienced the power of number one and are practicing this "surrender and win" principle.

This time the emergency is personal.

I'm still in my messy stage but have the sense to reach out to a

41 Marya Besharov, Wendy K. Smith, and Michael L. Tushman, "How Companies Can Balance Social Impact and Financial Goals, *Harvard Business Review*, January 4, 2019, https://hbr.org/2019/01/how-companies-can-balance-social-impact-and-financial-goals.

friend. I show up at his doorstep, and he invites me in. I spill my guts, and he listens to my torrent of self-pity. I finally run out of gas, and he asks a few questions. He's not gentle. In fact, I need to clean up his language to keep our PG rating.

"Do you have a car?" he asks. I nod yes. "Do you have a roof over your head?" Of course. "Have you eaten today?" Yes, again. I'm starting to feel awkward. He asks a couple more similar questions and then delivers the punch line. He looks me dead in the eye and shouts, "You are an asshole!" I feel like he's just slapped me in the face. "Don't you realize that you have more than 90 percent of the people in the world today? Why don't you take your sorry ass home, try to be grateful for once, and be back here at 9:00 a.m. tomorrow. Oh yeah, and don't drink."

His tough love was a shock to the system, for sure, but it worked and I've never forgotten what he told me. His words jolted me into gratitude, another strategy that contributed to my eventual letting go. Whatever it takes, right?

> *The really important kind of freedom involves attention, and awareness, and discipline.*
> **—DAVID FOSTER WALLACE**

Why do we open up to big, disruptive change, personally or in business? Because we must. It's never a casual thing; it's almost always an emergency. So instead of complaining and looking for someone to blame, including oneself, why not learn to appreciate what's happening for what it is, an alarm going off that can wake us up?

A TRUST EXERCISE

You can fill this out here or access it on our website, successparadox-book.com.

Pick a troublesome situation in your working life. Ask yourself: "What would be the biggest improvement that might happen if things really changed?" Take a moment to come up with something grand.

_____

_____

_____

_____

Next, ask yourself, what would need to happen for that to occur? Give that a good moment's thought.

_____

_____

_____

_____

Finally, ask: "What big change do I need to open up to, to facilitate this improvement?"

_____

_____

_____

_____

WHAT IF?

These are two powerful words. What if …? You can complete that sentence in countless ways. Experiment with asking the question when you feel trapped in some situation that resists change. What if?

If you're really brave, you might add this question:

If I weren't already doing this, would I choose to … today?

Exercise your imagination right now. Daydream about your life/ work, and see what shows up. Notice any negative thinking that arises and let it go. Simply hold your attention on the situation and actively wonder. This is a skill that came naturally to us as children, but we tend to grow out of it. We want to revive this skill.

> *I believe that dreams—day dreams, you know, with your eyes wide open and your brain-machinery whizzing— are likely to lead to the betterment of the world.*
>
> **—L. FRANK BAUM**

This chapter's paradox is supremely practical. It exposes the "greener grass" syndrome, how wanting something that's not present can blind us to resources that are staring us in the face. The big change we're speaking of is often less about the thing itself than it is about freeing ourselves from whatever is stopping us from embracing disruptive change.

For those who'd like some proof for just how practical this can be, watch a closing scene in the 1966 French film *King of Hearts* where Alan Bates's character is desperate to discover the location of a bomb that will obliterate the village at midnight. Meanwhile, Geneviève Bujold's love-struck character just wants to make out. He pushes her away repeatedly, finally crying out: "Don't you know we only have five minutes left?" She bats her long eyelashes and sighs, "Five minutes would be wonderful!" He gives up, collapses into her embrace and, a moment later, jumps up. "I've got it! I know where the bomb is!" He saves the town.

What he wanted—to figure things out—he couldn't get. What he needed—the answer to a perplexing question—was right there, lurking in his own mind. He found that answer when he surrendered. He let go of "trying" and relaxed into enjoying the moment with someone who just wanted to love him. In that moment of letting go, his mind opened to deliver him the answer. He got the girl and saved the town, incredible!

THE OPENING TO BIG CHANGE SCORECARD

You can fill this out here or access it on our website successsparadox-book.com.

For each statement below, check the appropriate box from 1 to 5: 1 for strongly no, 5 for absolutely yes, 2–4 for degrees in between. Trust your first intuitive answer.

	1	2	3	4	5
Do you easily make small course corrections day to day?					
Do the environments in your working life and family encourage openness to change?					
Do you treat colleagues, employees, and family members fairly, or does favoritism influence your behavior?					
Would you describe the mood at work and at home as one of gratitude?					
Are you traditionally open to big change without needing extreme pain or failure to motivate you?					

	1	2	3	4	5
Do your career choices follow the Lifestyle formula, prioritizing being authentic, doing good, then doing well, in that order?					
Have you experienced prioritizing doing good before doing well generating significant financial rewards?					
Are you willing to consider making big changes?					
Can you think of one big change to make, and are you willing to make it?					
Can you choose a first action step and commit to making it?					

Total each column, add them together, then multiply by two to determine your percent score.

DATE: _____   SCORE: _____

SCORING RESULTS (%)

0-25 Opening to big change is difficult for you. Use daydreaming like simulations to practice without consequences.

26-50 You can build on your successful experience of trusting and taking the leap into big change. Pick something in your life/work to experiment with.

51-75 You are comfortable with disruptive change. Think back on when you have taken unnecessary risks and see what you can learn about your habits. Adjust as necessary.

76-100   Big change doesn't threaten you. Run a quick inventory on your life/work to discover if there's anything you've been avoiding that you can work on.

Help!

High Is Low,
Low Is High

We'd rather feel high than low, right?

Social media can give us instant gratification, but at what price?

Addiction to quick hits of dopamine.

But real life can't be all highs and no lows.

Imagine a high being the underside of a vast joy.

Imagine a low being the top of a deep peace.

Imagine living between the two,

in a moving sea of meaning.

It's all good.

CHAPTER NINE

Answering a Cry for Help

Social media is biased, not to the Left or the Right, but downward. The relative ease of using negative emotions for the purposes of addiction and manipulation makes it relatively easier to achieve undignified results. An unfortunate combination of biology and math favors degradation of the human world.

—JARON LANIER

I'm six months sober, sitting on the beach taking a time-out from a business training. I've been in isolation for a couple of years now, a self-made prison of sorts where I'm experimenting with doing the opposite of what my habitual desires tell me to do. I feel like there are jumper cables attached to my nerve endings, amplifying all my emotions. I'd been numb for decades, but now the dam has burst. I'm not using any medications, so everything, even commercials on TV, makes me cry. I'm wide open, desperate to change how I run my businesses and how I live my life.

I sit in the sand and reflect. My entire career has been about "doing," full speed ahead and ignore the consequences. I didn't mind setting things on fire because I loved being the guy who puts out fires. I remember driving four hours for thirty-minute meetings. It was like riding in on a white horse, being the hero, the rescuer, the boss, the fixer, the "good guy." This was my way of life.

But now, as I sit and reflect, I realize this is not heroic at all; it's just another addiction. I need that adrenaline rush. It's how I've been running our family businesses for over twenty years.

A lightning thought strikes my mind: "I've failed. It's over."

Tears flow as I realize how long it's been since I just enjoyed being alive. When did I start playing God? I wonder.

Something happens.

I let go. I surrender. I give up. I'm waving a white flag. A strange kind of calm streams into my body.

I return to the meeting in time to hear the speaker of the day, Brett Pyle, telling stories from his book, Your Extraordinary Why. *He's mesmerizing! I catch him saying "… there he sits on his balcony in Paris above the Champs-Élysées sipping tea and reading a front-page obituary: 'the merchant of death is dead!'" I settle into my chair and listen.*

It's 1888, and this man's brother has just died. But all the news-papers thought it was him. So he's reading his own obituary! And this is what they're calling him, the Merchant of Death. Who is this man? Alfred Nobel. The Nobel Prize guy. So why the headline: "The Merchant of Death Is Dead"?

Alfred Nobel was a Swedish chemist who invented dynamite.

He'd intended it to help the building industry and provide a deterrent to war. In fact, his invention ignited a tsunami of weapon manufacturing. And now, here he was, confronted with his legacy—not that he helped mankind but that he would be remembered only as a war profiteer.

He was mortified. So am I! I listen, feeling like I'm right there on the balcony with Nobel and that I'm reading my own obituary too. How will I be remembered?

Brett Pyle continues telling Alfred Nobel's story. That moment changed Nobel's life forever. He crafted a new will, leaving 94 percent of his vast fortune to fund the Nobel Prize, awarded each year to those who "conferred the greatest benefit to mankind."[42]

I sit and wonder, "How can I change my legacy? How can I be remembered for something better?"

THAT QUESTION HAUNTED ME FOR YEARS. Young Jack's suicide shocked me into a sudden awareness, and I made an insightful connection: social media. Social media was like dynamite to me. It had been quietly destroying my sense of self, my life, *and* my business for over ten years. I'd tried to quit, I *had* quit, but it was another irresistible addiction, and I kept going back. How many people were just like me or worse?

Cyber void is so full of amazing emptiness that it makes us feel fulfilled.

—MUNIA KHAN

---

42   Wikipedia, "Alfred Nobel," https://en.wikipedia.org/wiki/Alfred_Nobel.

I was a late adopter, and Facebook was my platform of choice. It was euphoric in the beginning, catching up with friends, family, and college buddies I hadn't seen in fifteen years. Then my competitive nature took over. I started comparing myself and worrying about how many friends and likes I could get. Sound familiar?

Social media became another addiction, just like my drinking.

It started slow and innocent but got out of control fast. There was just too much positive reinforcement. "Gary, you're such a great guy; your family looks amazing; I love your sunsets and the beautiful flowers. You're such a great dad."

As my drinking got worse, so did my Facebook experience. It was a deadly combination, and it became obsessive. Social media intensified my chronic depression and anxiety for over a decade. I had regular panic attacks. I know the feeling of not being able to breathe. I took Xanax, I reached for another drink, I lived in denial, using workaholism and alcoholism and financial success to hide from the deep causes of those symptoms. And through it all, I obsessed on social media.

One morning, I got an urgent message from a friend to call him immediately. He told me that I had sent a few texts out the night before that didn't make much sense. I didn't remember doing that. This was my tipping point; I quit on the spot before it could get even worse.

I avoided the fate of someone I'd read about who got in a fight with his girlfriend, passed out naked on the couch, and woke up to discover that she had texted naked pictures of him from his phone to all his social media platforms. Ouch! Overnight, he became "that guy." That's how social media can ruin our lives, literally overnight. That's the reward for playing with dynamite!

> *Social media is like waking up in a mental asylum. You have no idea you're committed until you try to leave.*

These days I only use LinkedIn and have hired someone to manage it for me. When I found out about Nobel and dynamite, I thought about young Jack's suicide and the destructive effect of social media. But if social media was like dynamite, why couldn't it also be used for good, just like dynamite was?

> *If you can't stop thinking about someone's update,*
> *that's called "status cling."*
> **—JESSICA PARK**

THE GOOD

Social media connects us beyond geography. It's a great community-building tool. How many of us have been able to reconnect with old friends because of Facebook? Social media has also revolutionized marketing and education, enabling us to target customers and students who want what we are offering.

> *People who smile while they are alone used to be called insane,*
> *until we invented smartphones and social media.*
> **—MOKOKOMA MOKHONOANA**

Our ability to instantly connect with anyone anywhere has fundamentally altered our sense of the world, replacing geography with connectivity. A friend with a bad signal down the block is farther away than another friend three thousand miles away who has more bandwidth. Likewise, social media has shifted the nature of friendships. We stay close, not primarily to our best friends but to those who are using social media. That's not necessarily a good thing.

THE BAD

Social media is addictive. The instant gratification of a like or a retweet becomes candy/cocaine. Tastes good, feels great, more please, right now! We can belong, without having to look a certain way (Photoshop improves how we look). We don't need special or, more importantly, real-life social skills. We just type, click, and link.

> Social media is addictive. The instant gratification of a like or a retweet becomes candy/cocaine.

But ... we're seduced into a world of comparisons. How can we feel great about ourselves when others have more friends, get more likes, and when they look how we wish we looked (even though we know their pictures are probably photoshopped, just like ours are)? We're literally "making ourselves up," and so is everybody else, creating an online persona that's not who we are in real life, where we feel increasingly adrift.

What's worse, social media is a two-dimensional experience. We focus on a screen to the exclusion of the natural environment, which becomes an almost invisible backdrop for our life online. We become more visual and less kinesthetic. Because we're gazing at something flat, we flatten our emotional experience. Our ability to feel begins to atrophy, so we need more and more stimulation, which social media is happy to provide for extended periods of marketing and indoctrination.

Decades of mind control experiments conducted by the military confirmed that the key to manipulating someone was sensory deprivation. They used isolation techniques of various kinds. The modern equivalent is social media. When we're on our screens we're not in nature. The only sense we're using is sight, sometimes sound. So we're susceptible to whatever those invisible marketing puppeteers want us to absorb.

Using computers to reduce individual expression is a primitive,
retrograde activity, no matter how sophisticated your tools are.

—JARON LANIER

As of January 2022, over 58 percent of the world's population was using social media and the average daily usage was two hours and twenty-seven minutes.[43] When we omit babies, super seniors, and those with no access to electricity, and/or no ability to pay for access, that user number increases significantly. Almost everyone who can is using social media, and the percentages continue to climb. Two and a half hours online every day! How much time are we spending in nature every day?

Quoting from an online article at fastcompany.com: "We live on our phones and literally screen out the world. We're not fully cognitive and are on autopilot these days. It makes me wonder if we're inadvertently missing events that could prompt epiphanies."[44]

---

43   Dave Chaffey, "Global Social Media Statistics Research Summary 2022," Smart
      Insights, August 22, 2022, https://www.smartinsights.com/social-media-marketing/
      social-media-strategy/new-global-social-media-research/.

44   Stephanie Vozza, "This Is How to Have More Epiphanies," Fast
      Company, May 24, 2019, https://www.fastcompany.com/90353189/
      this-is-how-to-have-more-epiphanies.

THE EPIPHANY SOLUTION

The word "epiphany" is based on the same English word, which comes from the Greek *epiphaneia*, meaning "manifestation" or "appearance." In the grip of a genuine epiphany, we feel both powerful and helpless. An obvious example is sexual orgasm, impossible to control and never the same twice. That's the remarkable thing about letting go to an epiphany: something unknown that we can't control always happens.

The intellect has little to do on the road to discovery. There comes a leap in consciousness, call it intuition or what you will, the solution comes to you and you don't know how or why.

—ALBERT EINSTEIN

In my experience, epiphanies come in two flavors: random and earned. Random epiphanies just happen. They are like updrafts we catch, flowing through us, a sudden wind that elevates our experience. A sunset, a distant strain of music, a glance from a friend, a line of poetry, even the sudden tug on a fishing line. Something triggers an altered state of experience.

Earned epiphanies are less magical. They arise from self-regulation. We've all experienced these as well. After months of disciplined focus, a breakthrough happens. The joke in Hollywood is: "It only took me twenty years to become an overnight success!"

Social media offers a convenient but addictive and ultimately disempowering alternative to both: peak experiences on demand. Just click and read/watch/listen/share. Unfortunately, this makes us spectators, not participants, and certainly not heroes in our real lives.

It's hard to compete with instant gratification.

The psychologist Abraham Maslow described peak experiences this way:

- Feelings of limitless horizons opening up to the vision.

- The feeling of being simultaneously more powerful and also more helpless than one ever was before.

- The feeling of ecstasy and wonder and awe.

- The loss of placement in time and space.

- The conviction that something extremely important and valuable had happened, so that the subject was to some extent transformed and strengthened, even in his daily life by such experiences.[45]

Since life without peak experiences would be boring, how about using social media, not for instant gratification, but as a context for the regular experience of epiphanies? Not the quick-hit kind but the natural ones. We could focus on how to integrate them, to be transformed, not just temporarily stimulated.

Almost from page one, we've advocated for organizations to create environments that nurture everyone to become authentic. Now we're adding social media as another environment where the same personal benefits could develop. But this would require using social media personally the same way we leverage it in our businesses. Instead of being a compliant participant, unconsciously following whatever and whoever, we would ask: "How can I use these platforms to my personal advantage, not just for mindless distraction?"

This requires staying focused and resisting the temptation to go down the many rabbit holes that litter the social media landscape.

---

45   Rick Heyland, "Planning for Peak Experiences," ci4life.com, accessed July 19, 2022, https://ci4life.org/2020/08/05/planning-for-peak-experiences/.

Advice from *The Shrink for Entrepreneurs*:

> A ton of research is suggesting a growing problem in the Western world with our ability to self-regulate. Simply put, we're less disciplined and more prone to the traps of instant gratification and laziness than ever before.
>
> Something massive has shifted in our culture since Victorian times. Figuring out insights about ourselves is no longer enough to change our lives.[46]

This shines a searchlight into how we *shouldn't* be using social media. It's not about "me." It's about us, using this potentially great community-building and market technology for exactly that, not for navigating a swamp of self-esteem landmines with the vain hope of becoming more popular, more accepted, and "better."

THE POWER OF A WELL-POSITIONED FULCRUM

So how can we use social media for a worthy purpose beyond entertainment and fake friendship? Perhaps the answer to that question starts with asking another question: "Who's the boss?" Being online sets us up to be spectators. We read, we watch, we listen, and sometimes we respond. We're spellbound, hypnotized, and hours can fly by. AI is in charge. How could we reverse that relationship?

Being online sets us up to be spectators.

It starts with increasing our awareness of what's really going

---

[46] Andreas Komninos, "Self-Actualization: Maslow's Hierarchy of Needs," Interaction Design Foundation, accessed September 5, 2022, https://www.interaction-design.org/literature/article/self-actualization-maslow-s-hierarchy-of-needs#:~:text=Self%2Dactualization%20is%20the%20final,esteem%2C%20in%20that%20order.

on. Concentrating on some task, moments of rich solitude, and real conversations are being interrupted all day long by pings from our phones. This does enable us to stay in constant touch with our world and respond immediately. But it also disrupts our momentary experience. Someone is a puppet, and someone is pulling the strings. Who's who? What about our personal boundaries?

I watched an interesting video the other day entitled "A Fulcrum Ninja on Wall Street."[47] The presenter, Dr. David Martin, sketched out what happens when you place a fulcrum very close to what you want to move. It gives you much more leverage. Here's an image that describes our current attempt to make social media a more positive influence.

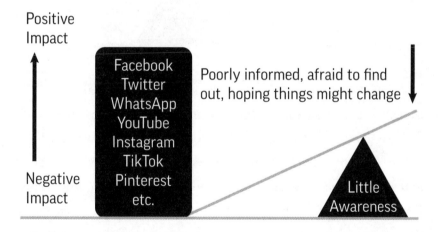

If you've ever tried to use a lever this way, you know how little leverage you have. Likewise, with only a distant awareness of the downsides of social media and what our kids are doing online, our desire to improve things is dust in the wind. We don't have much leverage.

---

47 David Martin, "A Fulcrum Ninja on Wall Street: David Martin at TEDxDelrayBeach," October 2, 2013, https://www.youtube.com/watch?v=9hW2zg-boQE.

Now, let's look at what happens when we move the fulcrum closer.

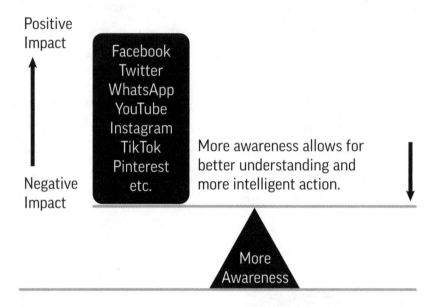

Social media can take over our lives when we make ourselves available to being seduced. It's a potent temptress! If we aren't consciously committed to our own vision, mission, and values, if we haven't surrendered to a higher power, if we aren't busy doing good and reaping the rewards … we're vulnerable. On the other hand, if we know we're in charge, and we determine to use social media to support what's important to us, then we don't shrink away and complain about what's wrong; we actually move closer to the problem, which we determine to convert into an asset. We might even use social media more, on this basis, but now it's fundamentally different. We're using it; it's not using us.

USING SOCIAL MEDIA SO IT DOESN'T USE US

1. Be the boss. Consciously choose when to go on and offline. There's no law against shutting off your phone and only turning it on for select periods each day (and informing your friends and colleagues that you're doing that). We used to have answering machines for our landlines, remember? That worked out just fine.

2. Focus first. Ask yourself why you're surfing, why you're going on Facebook, LinkedIn, etc.? What's your purpose in those moments, beyond distracting yourself from the tedium/challenges of your life?

3. Time limit. Decide how long you plan to be there, and set an alert on your phone if necessary.

4. Nature rules. Substitute time usually spent online for time spent in nature.

5. Buddy up. Ask a friend to be your social media buddy, someone you can reach out to if you're slipping back into addictive behaviors online.

What about emergencies? Fair enough. Everyone's situation is different, so each one of us has to figure out if it's realistic to periodically go offline. But here's something to think about. If we feel the need to keep our phones on all the time, "just in case," aren't we living in fear? Isn't that an expectation that something could go wrong?

Let's officially resign from the club where technology-driven connectivity has replaced our natural connections with each other, with nature, with all other life forms. Google is not God.

> *An authentic person connected to universal intelligence never abandons their sovereignty to artificial intelligence.*

HIGH IS LOW, LOW IS HIGH

Our paradox for this chapter is "High is low, low is high." When we feel "high," we are brushing up against the ceiling of a boundless heaven, the infinite potential of creative possibilities. So we're on the low end of that. When we feel "low," we are dipping our toe into the underworld of our unconscious mind, where, as Jung said, we become enlightened by making the darkness conscious.

My family has really helped me do that. Of course, you love all your kids, and you try not to have favorites, but that's hard. So I decided they could rotate. Today it's my daughter, Gracyn. Tomorrow it could be my eldest son, Clemons, or either of the other two boys, Marshall or Sutton.

Gracyn ... she's amazing. One of the most intelligent, interesting people I know. For a fact, I know I hurt her when I was going through my stuff, embarrassed her, maybe even humiliated her with her peer group. She's always had her own coping problems, so once I got a handle on mine, I figured I could help by telling her how to fix things, and even make decisions for her. Bad idea.

When her issues came to a head and she needed professional support, I realized the best help I could offer was to trust her. Something changed when I did that. She recovered, and we've developed the special daughter/father friendship we always wanted, knowing that we struggle with some of the same problems. Every day she reminds me that when you trust someone, it encourages them to prove they deserve it. She amazes me every day with her courage. She faces things I will never understand—nor do I need to—and she does it with fearlessness and grace. I know that we named her correctly.

SOCIAL MEDIA SCORECARD

Do this here or access via our website, successparadoxbook.com.

For each statement below, check the appropriate box from 1 to 5: 1 for strongly no, 5 for absolutely yes, 2–4 for degrees in between. Trust your first intuitive answer.

	1	2	3	4	5
Have you found your true calling in real life?					
Is social media a healthy activity in your life and business?					
Do you use social media to build communities of value?					
Are you ready and willing to create a better social media experience?					
Do you have significant epiphanies on a regular basis?					
Have you let go of always chasing the next high?					
Do you agree that gaining insights about yourself is not enough to produce transformation, that disciplined follow-through is also required?					
Are you comfortable asking for help when you need it?					

	1	2	3	4	5
Will you connect with a friend to become social media buddies?					
Can you come up with a first step to improve your experience with social media and commit to it?					

Total each column, add all five totals, then multiply by two to determine your percent score.

DATE: _____   SCORE: _____

SCORING RESULTS (%)

0-25   Giving up social media as unregulated entertainment is your first step.

26-50   You are beginning to monitor your social media "diet." Stay alert.

51-75   You are exerting control over your attention and making wise choices. Now it's time to get proactive and create intentions for how you use social media.

76-100   Social media is a positive force in your life. Help others make it so for them.

NEXT:

Healing our past.

We Can Change Our Past from the Future

We can't change the past, right?

Well ...

Einstein said that time is an illusion.

*Becoming authentic changes our behaviors,
and that changes our future.
We begin to see things differently, even our past.
Memories seem to change
when we look back at them through new eyes.*

It's never too late to have a happy childhood.

CHAPTER TEN

Healing Our Past

Simply touching a difficult memory with some slight willingness to heal begins to soften the holding and tension around it.

—STEPHEN LEVINE

The board meeting is starting. I arrive in a sweat, nervous and apprehensive. For good reason. An executive position has opened in our company, and someone wants that chair. He assumes it's his, but I know he's not the right choice. In fact, I've already chosen someone else and told them. What's more, I promised to phone the other guy to let him know, explain my choice, and process the disappointment ... before the meeting.

I "forgot" to do that. Right. The truth is, I chickened out.

The meeting starts, and I announce my choice. A bomb explodes in the room, at least for you know who. Months of conflict follow, all of which could have been avoided had I shown more respect for this person by making that call and working through what we needed to ahead of time.

WHO DOESN'T WISH they could rewind the tape of their lives and do a few things differently? "If I only knew then what I know now …" We've all sung that song. So, what do we do with our troublesome memories?

Life can only be understood backwards; but it must be lived forwards.
—SØREN KIERKEGAARD

Spanish philosopher George Santayana is credited with saying, "Those who cannot remember the past are condemned to repeat it," a sentiment echoed by Winston Churchill who wrote, "Those that fail to learn from history are doomed to repeat it." If we take these two together, the remedy for overcoming the tendency to "rinse and repeat" seems to be: remember and learn.

In his book, *Positive Intelligence: Why Only 20% of Teams and Individuals Achieve Their True Potential and How You Can Achieve Yours*, Shirzad Chamine explains the difference between explicit and implicit memories. Explicit are conscious, implicit are unconscious, stored away when the hippocampus in our brain goes offline, which it does in high-stress situations. He writes,

> It (the hippocampus) also is offline very early in our childhood, which is why some of the most powerful and important experiences of our lives that determine how we think and react to things are hidden from us.

> Researchers have shown that our implicit memories result in emotions and impact our decision making without our conscious awareness. We rationalize why we do what we do without being fully aware of the memories, feelings, and

assumptions that actually motivated our actions from our implicit storage.[48]

I'm the baby of the family, watching Saturday-morning cartoons with my three siblings. "Conjunction Junction, what's your function?" Dad comes down the stairs, and I dive under a quilt on the couch. He pulls the covers back, and I pretend to be asleep as he says, "Hey, Little Buck, want to ride with me today?"

We load up my mom's hand-me-down car and set off for a three-hour ride to one of his company's nursing homes in Columbia. When we arrive, he leads me past rooms where patients are tied down. Little old people in their soiled clothes are screaming and crying. We eat lunch in a lifeless cafeteria.

Driving home, he asks me, "Whacha gonna do when you get out of school?" Still disturbed from the encounter and too young to understand his vision to help these people receive better care right in their own homes, all I can think of is that I don't want to be the kid who comes home from college to work for his dad. But that's exactly what I ended up doing.

Childhood memories build a foundation for our lives.

I have so many happy memories of my family—playing with my brother and sisters, accompanying my father on road trips—plus my share of troublesome recollections, just like everyone else. None of us grow up untouched by parental imprints, some helpful and others, not so much. We all put together some kind of a decision-making

---

48 Shirzad Chamine, *Positive Intelligence: Why Only 20% of Teams and Individuals Achieve Their True Potential and How You Can Achieve Yours* (Austin, TX: Greenleaf, 2012), 216.

process that's rarely well constructed. So it's inevitable that we would lose touch with our authentic selves along the way.

My parents were kind and generous. I grew up in a wonderful home. I was more fortunate than most. But I was programmed, like every other kid, and I sure didn't receive any education or solid advice about how to become the fullness of myself.

Like most people who look back on their past, I have a long list of regrets. But I've learned a few ways to free myself from the burden of self-judgment about memories I can't change. It helps to decide that I actually chose my experiences back then and that I always did the best I could, given my age, my limitations, and the nature of the circumstances.

I've also accepted that everything happens for reasons we won't ever completely understand and that there are lessons in everything, if we choose to learn them. As I review my past and tour through the memories, I remind myself that I can always make a different choice today.

I want it.

It's a small insurance company, and I want to buy it. Coach Sharon has run assessments and told me it's not a good fit for us. But I want it anyway.

I force things. I invest weeks, playing with the numbers, trying everything I can to make it work. It doesn't. It can't. Sharon was right.

As I review my past and tour through the memories, I remind myself that I can always make a different choice today.

I finally pull the plug and walk away. I know I should have done that much earlier. Why was I so stubborn? And what do I do now, with all this remorse and self-judgment?

I've shared enough business screw-up stories for you to get some idea of how many memories of failure I must be carrying around. But memories of failure don't support us to succeed in the future. Caroline Beaton, writing for Forbes.com, explains:

> When animals, be they tadpole or human, win at something, their brains release testosterone and dopamine. With time and repetition, this signal morphs the brain's structure and chemical configuration to make successful animals smarter, better trained, more confident and more likely to succeed in the future. Biologists call it the Winner Effect.

> The not-yet-named Loser Effect is equally cyclical: contrary to Nietzsche's adage, what doesn't kill you often makes you weaker. In one study, monkeys who made a mistake in a trial—even after mastering the task on par with other monkeys—later performed worse than monkeys who made no mistakes. "In other words," explains *Scientific American*, they were "thrown off by mistakes instead of learning from them." Some research similarly suggests that failure can impede concentration, thereby sabotaging future performance.[49]

How much you can learn when you fail determines
how far you will go into achieving your goals.

—ROY BENNETT

Beaton goes on to offer three helpful strategies:

---

49 Caroline Beaton, "This Is What Happens to Your Brain When You Fail (And How to Fix It)," *Forbes*, April 7, 2016, https://www.forbes.com/sites/carolinebeaton/2016/04/07/this-is-what-happens-to-your-brain-when-you-fail-and-how-to-fix-it/.

- Instead of dwelling on a failure, reframe it as something less weighty. Maintain a positive mindset and choose optimism.

- Don't wing it. It's tempting to leap into novelty, but it's more effective to develop "highly specific, far-reaching goals."

- Don't threaten yourself. "Do this right or you'll end up like last time" generates anxiety. Instead, celebrate small wins.

This may sound strange, but we actually only remember something once. From then on, we remember our most recent recollection, and that "memory" keeps changing. Obviously so, because *we* are changing over time, so we "remember" through a mind that keeps evolving.

The result is like that campfire story game. What's whispered to me changes as I try to relay what I thought I heard to you, and on it goes around the circle, the story getting altered in every retelling. Likewise, our memories change slightly with every recall. When there's trauma attached and we were a powerless victim, the remembering ritual can become a rehearsal for future failures.

That's not a good formula for creating business success or personal happiness.

I've really done it this time, something so utterly wrong that I'm sure my wife and family will never forgive me.

I sit in the darkened hotel room, drinking and crying and beating myself up.

We're $3 million in debt, and the IRS wants another $500,000. I feel completely humiliated and can't imagine a road back from this hell. So, what do I do now, when all I can think about is escaping?

E. B. Johnson blogs, "If you've betrayed someone, it's imperative that you learn how to understand the patterns and triggers that bring you to your worst impulses. Stop hurting the people you love and start getting honest with yourself and the world, in order to create a future you can actually be proud of. You'll never be happy until you learn how to trust in yourself and others, but you have to make a commitment and put in the work to get there."[50]

It is easier to forgive an enemy than to forgive a friend.

—WILLIAM BLAKE

Johnson describes "the work" this way:

1. Open up: Confront and admit to what happened, how you are feeling, and offer a heartfelt apology.

2. Make an honesty pact: Commit to an honest and open future.

3. Answer the questions: It's easy to get defensive when confronted with a serious misstep.

4. Stop invalidating the feelings of others: Listen. Don't tell someone they are being unreasonable or they don't understand. Respect how they are feeling, whether it seems realistic to you or not.

5. Practice patience: Regaining trust takes time. Apologies just begin the healing process.

---

50 E. B. Johnson, "If You've Betrayed Someone You Love This Is How to Come Back," *Practical Growth*, November 12, 2019, https://medium.com/practical-growth/how-to-come-back-from-betraying-someone-b3bf04e5d828.

6. Stop making excuses and start taking responsibility: You did what you did. There's no one else to blame. Admit you made a choice and make a better one now.

7. Focus on recovery, rather than results: Be patient with the recovery process and stay with the journey.

A "FORGIVING BETRAYAL" REHEARSAL

1. Think of a betrayal memory you'd like to experiment on.

2. Imagine a dialogue with the person(s) involved.

3. Simulate back-and-forth comments, resisting the temptation to be defensive or explain yourself. Notice yourself listening.

4. Admit you made a choice that went bad; commit to making better choices.

There's no risk to this imaginative simulation exercise, and experimenting can build your confidence to engage in real-time forgiveness conversations. Whenever I've done this, I've almost always found that the other party was totally willing to put the memory of injury to rest.

I've been able to change many of the habits that caused my missteps in the past. The happiness and harmony I experience today is a strong proof of the value of surrendering control and trusting a higher power to run my life. If only I'd known this secret decades ago! For sure, I'll still be talking about this and learning myself, many decades from now. Relationships are everything, for better and for worse.

How you correct your mistakes will define your
character and commitment to a higher power.

—SHANNON L. ALDER

When it comes to memories of abuse, therapists understand that healing often requires surfacing our anger, then navigating through it to feel and release the grief buried underneath. A friend relayed his experience in a men's workshop where someone noticed scars on one man's arm and asked about it. "Oh, those are where my father stubbed out his cigarettes and cigars."

After a moment of shocked silence, the facilitator inquired, "You know that's not OK, right?" Supported by the others, this man was able to connect with and vent his rage, then drop deep into his grief. A torrent of tears later, he collapsed in the corner, emptied and renewed. He reported later that this became a landmark turning point in his life.

HO'OPONOPONO

My writing partner lives in Hawaii. He practices a traditional forgiveness ritual called the ho'oponopono[51] prayer, which is composed of four sentiments: "I'm sorry, please forgive me, thank you, I love you." It's a kind of lullaby to the self, to address troublesome memories when they arise.

"I'm sorry" is the first essential step, admitting that I made a mistake, that I hurt someone, and I regret it. "Please forgive me" is an expression of humility and remorse, a request for forgiveness from a position of surrender. "Thank you" expresses appreciation for

---

51 Admin, "Understanding Ho'oponopono: A Beautiful Hawaiian Teaching About Forgiveness," Grace and Lightness, January 25, 2022, https://graceandlightness.com/hooponopono-hawaiian-prayer-for-forgiveness/.

whatever comes back from the other person. Finally, "I love you" affirms the choice I'm making now. Whatever the injury, this is what I want now, love to share, with no strings attached.

> Hoʻoponopono can be performed any time with any person, often done when they are not present. You might consider making a list of remembered incidents where you hurt others. Then bring each person to mind, one at a time, and direct the prayer toward them.

You could try this right now. Think of someone you hurt in the past, picture them in your mind, and silently say these words, making sure to pause as you go so you can really feel the meaning of what you are saying:

I'm sorry,

Please forgive me,

Thank you,

I love you.

ACTIONS SPEAK LOUDER THAN WORDS

I write letters to our four children from rehab. When I get out, Kelly invites me to the beach house. The kids are there. Three of them are immediately kind and welcoming. But Marshall, who has always had a strong sense of right and wrong, won't look at me and won't talk to me.

On our own in the kitchen, Kelly notices the sadness on my face and asks what's wrong. I share my grief about Marshall and she says, "Well, he doesn't want to talk to you. He doesn't care what you say. He's going to watch what you do!"

I immediately think of something my friend Mark had told me about rebuilding damaged relationships: just keep your word.

Marshall likes pizza from Landofis, a nearby Italian place. So Friday becomes pizza night. There are many Fridays when everyone goes somewhere else, but I still get that pizza. It takes about a year before Marshall and I begin talking again. The "time-out" felt like eternity, but I'm grateful for the healing space it provided.

I didn't try to be a hero or do anything big. I didn't try to say the right things. I just picked up the pizza every Friday night. Today, our relationship has never been better.

Any man can be a father, but it takes someone special to be a dad.

—ANNE GEDDES

Marshall and I managed to heal our separateness. That counts for a lot because he has a high sense of morality. He doesn't say much, but when he does, it really means something. We laughingly refer to him as "the silent assassin." He just quietly does his thing. Like being number one at almost everything he tries. Bicycle kicks playing soccer when he was eight, straight As, and becoming number two hundred of about twenty million players on Fortnite. We're friends again now, and that's a miracle to me.

Maybe healing our past could be simpler than we think. Just develop new constructive habits—like getting pizza every Friday night for a while—stick with them, and refuse to identify as a victim whenever we remember something with regret.

> That was then; this is now. The past is gone. We're choosing the future we want and creating it, one smart choice at a time.

Our paradox in this chapter is "We can change our past from the future." Clearly, if we don't change habits, we'll keep creating today what we created yesterday, and our past will *become* our future. But when we prioritize being true to ourselves, our changed behaviors create a different future. This enables us to reflect back on our past with a more mature understanding. That's how we can change our past from the future.

HEALING OUR PAST SCORECARD

Fill this out here or access on our website, successparadoxbook.com.

For each statement below, check the appropriate box from 1 to 5: 1 for strongly no, 5 for absolutely yes, 2–4 for degrees in between. Trust your first intuitive answer.

Total each column, add all five totals, then multiply by two to determine your percent score.

	1	2	3	4	5
Can you look back on memories of personal error and feel deep, genuine regret?					
Are you willing to review your past to remember and learn?					
Do you agree that you chose your childhood experiences?					
Are you willing to learn how to clean up your memories, then do it?					
Do you agree that our memories change over time?					
Can you connect with acts of betrayal you have committed and instances where you have been betrayed and consider offering forgiveness to others and yourself?					
Are you ready to take the healing journey through anger to grief to forgiveness?					
Will you begin experimenting with the Hawaiian ho'oponopono forgiveness process?					
Do you agree that actions are more important than words, and will you examine your life to discover where you are not walking your talk?					
Do you agree that we can change our memories and that it is never too late to have a happy childhood?					

DATE: _____   SCORE: _____

SCORING RESULTS (%)

0-25   Memories are a problem for you. You have a choice, continue to be troubled by them or learn to change how you remember them.

26-50   You have some experience of examining your memories. Practice the exercise.

51-75   You've had some experience with how malleable memories are. Make an inventory of those you'd like to change. Explore and learn.

76-100   You are a memory master. Reviewing bothersome memories and healing them is a healthy habit for you already. You're ready to confront the truly traumatic ones.

NEXT:

Heading into Part Three, you'll strategize how to adopt the SPL, both for your business and in your life.

*If your system no longer delivers
the results you want, don't go for
incremental changes; instead go for
complete transformation.*

-ABHISHEK RATNA

PART THREE

*Taking action isn't a blind pursuit. Wise action means we're
guided by all our principles. We need to test and question
ourselves. We can be sure that we're on the right track when
our actions are guided by our principles. Wise action requires
that we listen to the truth as we pursue our passion.*

—HOWARD BEHAR, STARBUCKS

Reality Is an Act of Creation ... Yours

Is reality objective or subjective?

Why do things happen the way they do?

We are not spectators; we are creators.

And the best creating tool we have is our mind.

CHAPTER ELEVEN

What's Next for You?

Imagination gives us the opportunity to envision new possibilities—it is an essential launchpad for making our hopes come true. It fires our creativity, relieves our boredom, alleviates our pain, enhances our pleasure, and enriches our most intimate relationships. When people are compulsively and constantly pulled back into the past, to the last time they felt intense involvement and deep emotions, they suffer from a failure of imagination, a loss of their mental flexibility. Without imagination there is no hope, no chance to envision a better future, no place to go, no goal to reach.

—BESSEL VAN DER KOLK, MD

MY WIFE, KELLY, AND I HAVE BEEN TOGETHER for almost thirty years. Any of you in long-term marriages with kids know the challenges you face, even if one of the partners isn't a wing nut like I was. Along the same line, Kelly isn't exactly your typical wife. She is loud, funny, inappropriate at times, and loyal, and she has a huge bark but very little bite. Most people only see that, but those closest to her—like me, her family at large, select friends, and most of all our kids—experience her enormous heart. It's a heart with no beginning and no end for those she

193

truly cares for.

Without her love and loyalty, we certainly wouldn't still be married. I probably wouldn't even be alive to share my story and recommend this lifestyle for you. Kelly has been patient and forgiving, and, most of all, she's been totally honest. There was a lot of tough love coming my way from her during those dark years, and I deserved every bit of it. In fact, I feel it's the sign of deep friendship, being able to share the truth with each other, especially when it's painful. I know it's a familiar movie line, but I can say with total conviction that Kelly really has helped me become a better man.

I only hope that I've somehow helped her become a better woman. As the proverb says, "iron sharpens iron." It's uncomfortable, and there are sparks! Needless to say, there has never been a dull moment (pun intended).

I'm mentioning this here at the beginning of this chapter on what's next for you because it's so important to heal and enjoy our most important relationship, which is usually with our spouse. There are no accidents in who we spend our lives with, and partners can become our best teachers. God is a mischievous matchmaker!

I'm reading through a draft of this manuscript, studying what my writing partner, Will, and I have created. It's humbling to read and also a little daunting. I wonder, putting it out there like this ... I'm on the spot now to keep walking the talk. I guess that's a side benefit of writing a book. You're accountable.

Heading into the last three chapters, where we've decided to focus on how to apply all these lessons and insights, I'm recalling the many moments along the way when I really had given up hope. I remember feeling so worthless that I questioned going on.

I don't know if you've ever hit rock bottom like that. It's easy to forget that we have value when we're depressed, failing at life big time, screwing up our relationships, and maybe having a business that's tanking, with bankers harassing you for money.

All those memories of utter discouragement motivate me now. I was lucky. I got the help and support that I needed. I hope you do too. Remember that someone cares about you. Someone needs you. Don't give up.

Buckminster Fuller wrote: "Never forget that you are one of a kind. Never forget that if there weren't any need for you in all your uniqueness to be on this earth, you wouldn't be here in the first place. And never forget, no matter how overwhelming life's challenges and problems seem to be, that one person can make a difference in the world. In fact, it is always because of one person that all the changes that matter in the world come about. So be that one person."

> There are no accidents in who we spend our lives with, and partners can become our best teachers.

I've been blessed by more than a few "one person" individuals. I was at my lowest in terms of self-esteem when my pastor told me that "God doesn't make junk." He got about six inches from my face and asked me if there was anything my kids could do to make me not love them. My answer was an immediate and emphatic "No!"

He got even closer and literally shouted in my face: "That's how much God loves you, and you didn't have to do or accomplish anything to earn His love!" In the intensity of that moment, I couldn't resist saying, "Well, damn, I sure wasted a lot of time working hard for nothing then!"

Self-worth is a birthright, not a reward.

This is the great secret we seek to reveal in these pages. All of us are alive for a reason. Our purpose is to discover that reason and then fulfil it. As Pablo Picasso said, "The meaning of life is to find your gift. The purpose of life is to give it away."

Business is where I give my gifts, and it may be the same for you, or you may thrive doing something completely different like music or dance or snowboarding! If our educational systems were what they should be, our uniqueness would be encouraged, not constrained, and we'd learn how to give our gifts for the betterment of society.

Achieve your own greatness through your own uniqueness. Be a leader.

—SEBASTIEN RICHARD

With this priority in place, you can build a strategic plan for your personal life. That's what this chapter is for. The next chapter will do the same for your organization.

MIND THE MIND

You're going to need tools to create your preferred future, then learn how to construct it. Your most incredible tool, one that you already possess, is your mind. There are two more. Of course, tools must be used the right way to have value. Unfortunately, none of us were taught how the mind is designed to work.

Picture the conscious mind as a water wheel with paddles that receive water that pours down from above and moves the wheel, then cascading water down into a cistern below that overflows.

The wheel represents our conscious mind. The water is the flow of universal intelligence, God constantly communicating with us, we could say. The cistern symbolizes our subconscious mind, full of all we've learned, like language and skills, our memories, etc. So, universal intelligence activates the conscious mind, which selects material from our subconscious to give form to the invisible spirit of life, represented by the overflow out of that cistern.

WHAT HAPPENS WHEN WE PUT "BEING" FIRST

INSPIRED EXPRESSION

Conscious mind open to turn, inspired by life.

Universal Intelligence Flowing

Life inspired ideas and motivations

Harmony

Ever-Refreshing Memories Skills Imagination

Subconscious mind (Stimulated)

This model shows the conscious mind being activated by God (universal intelligence), which is the way we're designed to operate. We know this instinctively and use the term "going with the flow" to describe the ideal experience.

Now let's see what happens when that connection with universal intelligence is blocked. This happens when we prioritize doing over being and use our willpower, disconnected from the source of life—often with the best of intentions—but we know where paving that road leads.

WHAT HAPPENS WHEN WE PUT "DOING" FIRST

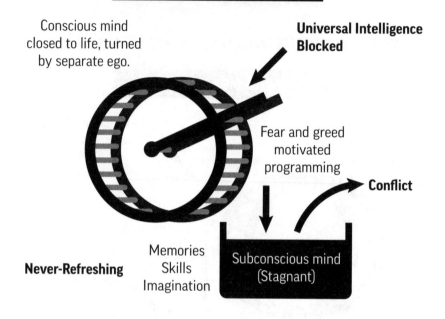

SELFISH EXPRESSION

Conscious mind closed to life, turned by separate ego.

Universal Intelligence Blocked

Fear and greed motivated programming

Conflict

Never-Refreshing

Memories
Skills
Imagination

Subconscious mind (Stagnant)

This illustrates why our connection with a higher power is so vital. This is not a religious concept; it's not just a virtuous quality. It's a necessity, *if* our minds are to operate properly to help us live lives of meaning and enjoyment. Without the inspiration from "above," we resort to cleverness and, as scripture says about the disconnected man, "Every imagination of the thoughts of his heart was only evil continually."

Resign your destiny to higher powers.

—WILLIAM JAMES

We've never been educated on how to use our minds this way, so we have a lifetime of experience cranking them around while blocking universal intelligence, to the point where many doubt that "it" even exists. God has become a religious belief, or the universe is seen as a giant clockwork machine, set in motion eons ago (by what or who, I wonder?) and operating on autopilot ever since. But proof of a governing, endlessly creative intelligence is indisputable, for those who have eyes to see.

The conscious mind is God's instrument
for transmitting divine wisdom into the world.

CREATING YOUR MAP TO THE FUTURE

Back in the Introduction, we invited you to come up with a word or two to define yourself, write it on a small piece of paper, and stick it in your wallet or purse. If you did that, now is the time to retrieve it.

How did you describe yourself back then? Would you still use those words, or would you choose something else, and what other qualities would you add? Here's an example of what we call a "Quality Profile," one person's qualities matched with behaviors to help them further develop and express each quality.

QUALITY	ENHANCING BEHAVIORS
Lighthearted	Finding something positive in every situation.
Kind	Listening to others, caring about their suffering.
Attentive	Inquiring, asking questions, noticing what's happening.
Fun	Telling jokes, being friendly.
Creative	Trying new things, using the imagination.
Curious	Setting aside assumptions, opening the mind.
Generous	Giving and receiving with gratitude.

This Quality Profile is someone's map to their future. Unlike any map you've ever seen, right? It's a "being map" for the mind, not a doing map for achievement.

Our future is built according to who we are, giving our creative gifts to increase value in our communities.

What qualities would you identify that describe you at your best? Fill out your list below, use a separate sheet of paper, or print out the form supplied on our website. Access through our website, successparadoxbook.com. We recommend doing this regularly to track your progress.

Can you be anything you want to be or you are already everything you want to be?

—SHUNYA

YOUR QUALITY PROFILE

QUALITY   ENHANCING BEHAVIORS

_____   _____

_____   _____

_____   _____

_____   _____

_____   _____

_____   _____

Memorize these qualities and practice repeating them to yourself as often as you like. For instance, the person in our example would say, "I am lighthearted, kind, attentive, fun, creative, curious, and generous." The more you affirm these qualities, the more you reprogram your brain to wire in these beliefs and express those qualities. They will naturally evolve over time as you become who you believe yourself to be, deepening the connection with your authentic self, the unique person you have always been.

We're telling you to start talking to yourself?

You're already doing that.

"Dr. Julia Harper, an occupational therapist and life coach, agrees that it's normal for us to talk to ourselves, but stresses that it's important to do it the right way. 'Self-talk is a normal part of the development of language,' she says. '[It improves our] higher order cognitive and meta-cognitive skills and is a fundamental part of self-mastery. Because of its functionality, not only do we all self-talk, it would behoove us to do it well.' "[52]

Remember that positive self-talk is an intrinsic part of a healthy mind.

—ASA DON BROWN

Doing it well means positive self-talk. Debbie Hampton, blogging for the Best Brain Possible, writes, "Many of us do repetitive exercises to improve our physical health, and affirmations are like exercises for our mind and outlook. These positive mental repetitions can reprogram your thinking patterns. Over time and with repeti-

---

52   Wendy Rose Gould, "Go Ahead, Talk to Yourself. It's Normal—and Good for You," Better By Today, October 9, 2018, https://www.nbcnews.com/better/health/talking-yourself-normal-here-s-how-master-it-ncna918091.

tion, you can begin to think and act differently. It's really just about becoming aware of and changing the way you talk to yourself."[53]

CREATING YOUR COMPASS FOR LIFE

Imagine having a compass to help you reach your goals in life. Here's an experiential process you can use right now to create it. There's an audio program for this exercise on our website.

Find a quiet, private spot and clear ten minutes in your day where you won't be interrupted. Door closed, phone off. Take a few deep breaths, pausing as you read, and feel your whole body relax. Pause to breathe.

. . .

Pick a day a year from now. Imagine where you would like to be. Picture yourself in that place on that day. Close your eyes for a moment and visualize it in detail.

. . .

Engage your senses. Where are you, exactly? On your deck, lying on a beach, sitting in your office? What time of day is it? What's the temperature? Who else is there? What can you hear and smell? What are you touching? Take enough time to create this environment in your mind, as detailed as possible (you'll get better with practice).

. . .

---

53   Debbie Hampton, "The Neuroscience of How Affirmations Help Your Mental Health," The Best Brain Possible, December 22, 2019, https://thebestbrainpossible.com/affirmations-brain-depression-anxiety/.

Begin daydreaming about what you would like your life to be like then. You can make up whatever you want. Let your imagination roam wide. Think about your living situation, your relationships, any possibilities for change you are wondering about. Dream big.

...

Now, imagine that what you are visualizing is real. Speak silently in the present tense, celebrating what you accomplished in one year. For instance, "I'm so glad our marriage is working better again, that the kids are doing well in school, that we paid off that second mortgage, that our business is turning a good profit." Speak in the present tense, as if these things have already happened.

...

The third and last step: How are you feeling? As you imagine this future reality, believing that you have already accomplished what you wish, how do you feel? Explore a range of emotions and settle on one or two words, as precise as possible. Yes, you will be happy, but make it more specific. How about ecstatic or grateful or joyful? Say it: "I feel ... "

...

This is how you will bring this vision into your real life, using your imagination to create seeds that will grow into the garden of your future. The feeling you identified provides the environment for those seeds to grow in.

Enjoy experimenting with this process on specific goals you would like to achieve.

You just gained three tools for creating your future:

1. Your mind (working the correct way).

2. A thinking map (your qualities of being).

3. A feeling compass (your vision of accomplished doing).

You can use your mind, your map, and your compass to navigate life, tuning in to that future feeling and changing your brain with those self-esteem statements. This will keep you flowing with that higher-power intelligence.

> *You will know what to think, feel, say, and do, guided by your mind flowing wisdom from a divine source.*

THREE ESSENTIALS

Using your mind, map, and compass to become an expert with the SPL requires commitment and follow-through. To stay motivated, we recommend three essentials:

1. Doing the practices regularly.

2. Partnering with a Success Paradox Buddy.

3. Engaging with the Success Paradox network.

Start where you are. Use what you have. Do what you can.

—ARTHUR ASHE

THE PRACTICES

You can refresh your memory by referencing prior chapters. You can also find these practices grouped together on our website, successparadoxbook.com.

PRACTICE	LOCATION
Mirror exercise	Chapter One
Morning time-out with breathing and father work	Chapter Two
Evening review	Chapter Three
Money game	Chapter Four
Morning, noon, evening meditations	Chapter Six
Lifestyle tracking system	Chapter Seven
Ho'oponopono forgiveness exercise	Chapter Ten
Personal quality profile	Chapter Eleven
Surrender exercise	Chapter Thirteen

PARTNERING WITH A SUCCESS PARADOX BUDDY

The best teachers are lifelong students. Find a buddy to teach who can teach you back. You might want to find a friend who is interested in the book. Give her a copy, and if she gets into it, set up a monthly date to discuss a chapter. Visit our website to learn about more options and about how to connect with a Success Paradox Buddy.

The best teachers are lifelong students.

ENGAGING WITH OUR NETWORK

We've set up a community support network you can access through our successparadoxbook.com.

Strong people don't put others down ... They lift them up.

—MICHAEL P. WATSON

STRUCTURAL TENSION

Peter Drucker famously said, "The best way to predict the future is to create it." We'll go one step further and propose: "The best way to create the future is to live it." In other words, to experience the future as a present reality. Why? Because it creates inner conflict. When your subconscious mind believes something (like the future you are pretending is already real), it will immediately begin working to resolve the perceived conflict between that vision and your current reality. All kinds of resources will start showing up to resolve that inner conflict by evolving your present to match your imagined future.

In his groundbreaking book, *The Path of Least Resistance*, Robert Fritz introduced the concept of structural tension to describe how this works. "When you form structural tension, it can be resolved one of two ways: toward the fulfillment of your vision as a reality, or toward the continuation of the reality you now have."[54]

He further elaborates by imagining a rubber band stretched between your thumb and forefinger. The thumb represents your current reality. Your forefinger symbolizes the future you wish to create. Stretched out, the tension in the rubber band must eventually resolve in one direction or the other. Depending on which finger holds strong, it will move in that direction. Stay focused on your vision for the future and your current reality will evolve into it.

---

54   Robert Fritz, *The Path of Least Resistance* (New York: Fawcett Books, 1989), 117.

People like us, who believe in physics, know that the distinction between past, present and future is only a stubbornly persistent illusion.

—ALBERT EINSTEIN

SUMMARY

1. You've learned how the conscious and subconscious minds work together under the direction of universal intelligence.

2. You've created your map and your compass.

3. You've developed structural tension between the way things are now and your vision for a preferred future.

Universal wisdom + Imagination + Commitment + Perseverance = Success.

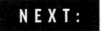

What's next for your organization?

Believing Is Seeing

Seeing is believing, right?

Well … it turns out that the opposite is also true.

*"Implicit bias" is the official term that describes how
our brains can blind us to the obvious,
when what we are looking for is in conflict
with what we believe we should see.*

Change beliefs, change perception.

CHAPTER TWELVE

What's Next for Your Organization?

Individual and organizational purpose go hand in hand. One needs the other to flourish. Most of today's organizations are primarily concerned with self-preservation and the bottom line, hardly a good setting for people to explore their calling. In such a setting, employees also view work in terms of self-preservation—a way to get a paycheck that pays the bills.

In contrast, when colleagues are invited to listen in to their organization's purpose, they are likely to wonder about their personal calling too: Does the organization's purpose resonate with me? Is this a place I feel called to work? What do I really feel called to do at this moment in my life? Will this place allow me to express my selfhood? Will it help me grow and develop?

—FREDERIC LALOUX

IF YOU'RE A BUSINESS OWNER, this will probably be your favorite chapter, because it dials in to exactly how we turned ours around and

209

how you can transform yours. If you're not a business owner, you might find this chapter irrelevant. Except, you know business owners. Consider giving one of them the book, or at least sharing this chapter.

I'm twenty-six, working in my father's company. He gives me plenty of room to learn from experience, and employees begin coming to me, rather than to him. He funds buying our companies but never gives me money for cashflow.

He visits every Friday. One week I'm short on payroll. I tell him, and it's a big deal. He had to notice my anxiety but asks about something else.

"What's going on with Sally?" he asks. Sally is the payroll clerk.

"What?" I'm totally confused. "Didn't you hear me? We're $100K short!"

"I heard that," he replies smoothly. "But Sally looks like she's upset." I don't know what he's talking about. "I get it," he continues. "Payroll is important. That's the big stuff. But if you take care of the small stuff, the big stuff will take care of itself." He smiles. "Find out what's going on with Sally. I think she needs your help."

Bullshit. That's what I think. Sally is just having a bad day. This guy has lost his marbles.

Years later, I come to understand what he was saying. I had to learn it the hard way, but now I know. I take care of little old ladies, and they fight for me. Payroll stops being a problem. I couldn't see what he saw, until I changed what I believed, and that only happened when I experienced the wisdom in what he saw for myself.

You may think, having read this far, that you'll have to make big changes to turn your organization around. You probably will. But it all starts with the decision to go for it, and each change involves a series of incremental steps. Here's what we did at Palmetto. I'll run through our turnaround process fast, then pull out the key strategies for you to customize and apply to your organization.

2011: We buy Palmetto Infusion.

2012–2016: We rally the company from $90,000 monthly losses to $100,000 monthly profit.

Our CEO dies unexpectedly. In a controversial move, David Goodall (prior CFO) replaces him.

2017: The company is operating in silos. Departments are run by stockholders who feel entitled as owners to regular cash disbursements, including me, whether they are well qualified or not and regardless of performance.

A broker values the company at $20 million, but the owners don't want to sell. This is our green light to start making significant changes.

The year 2017 was when I went through my dark night of the soul and emerged a changed man. I've already gone over my personal process. Here's what we did in the company.

We knew that we needed to grow beyond South Carolina and become a regional player. But we also knew that we had to get rid of the dysfunction first. That had already started with me.

We chose to incentivize growth. We put together a three-year strategic plan and rolled out a compensation program that rewarded stakeholders for performance. Some caught the vision and got motivated; others didn't. A few left the company; others changed positions.

> It all starts with the decision to go for it, and each change involves a series of incremental steps.

One day, a staff member wrote up one of the owners for doing something inappropriate. This was like dropping a nuclear bomb on the leadership team but in a good way. That simply couldn't have happened even a few months before or without me kicking it off. There had to be an obvious, visible proof of change at the top … and that was me.

If you are not willing to risk the unusual,
you will have to settle for the ordinary.

—JIM ROHN

Based on a recommendation from our head of HR, we hired Sharon Randaccio, an M&A and turnaround specialist with a deep background in commercial banking who coaches high-performing CEOs through Vistage International. She helped us turn those silos into teams by asking our directors and managers the right questions (in one-on-one meetings):

- What motivated them personally?
- What did they like about the company?
- What did they believe was best for patients?

From these dialogues, we developed language to describe our vision, mission, and values. It was a great day when the leadership team of fifteen said, "Yes, this is who we are!"

It became crystal clear: this is where we're going, and this is how we're going to get there. Everyone was emotionally aligned and got behind the plan. It was a three-year plan, but we hit our numbers in less than two years.

One of our best practices? Constant, transparent communication.

That included budget meetings, to track progress and stay aligned with the plan. But we spent less time on the numbers and more time on the vision, mission, and core values. Sharon helped us understand that this is what would drive patient experience. In turn, their deep engagement and emotional connection with our company drove profit.

In 2019 we adopted the EOS scorecard system developed by Gino Wickman (see his great book *Traction*). Every department got their own scorecard that tracked three or four quarterly goals for departments and individuals, all tied to annual bonuses. Hit your goals, get your bonus.

Everyone felt motivated to perform better, and that required collaboration because individual or department goals were at least partially dependent on other individuals and departments. Everyone in senior leadership got to see everyone else's scorecard, and progress was updated in weekly meetings.

The single most important ingredient in the recipe for success is transparency because transparency builds trust.

—DENISE MORRISON

We developed a succession plan for all senior leaders and a new employee orientation process, we updated employee performance standards to include engagement and values, and we conducted regular employee surveys.

Compliance was enthusiastic, with company-wide follow-through, and the growth we'd understood was essential to sustained success happened. We began opening new centers, and this really took off in 2019. We were growing exponentially, and our momentum coincided with a major stroke of luck: Blue Cross in South Carolina made a fortuitous (for us) policy decision. They disallowed patients from getting their infusions at hospitals because of excessive fees. This redirected all that business to us. The same phenomenon occurred beyond South Carolina, where we had just opened new centers.

The timing couldn't have been better.

Sharon helped us restructure our senior leadership team. We created a chief sales and marketing officer, a chief real estate officer, and invented a new position: business development director. This went to Tim Hayes, a longtime partner who managed to adapt, just like many of our other amazing partners did. Tim is a brilliant sales guy operating out of Greenville, and his critical thinking skills are through the roof. He'd go into an area and research it thoroughly, coming back with a report that either recommended or cautioned against opening a new center in that location. Every location he championed that we developed has done very well.

How did we handle the warp-speed growth? We hired more talent; immediately integrated them into our vision, mission, and values; and created more infrastructure. We had to stay ahead of the curve, so we put people in place early, even overhiring at times to ensure a consistently positive patient experience.

That's what mattered most to us and always will. Are we delivering value to our patients, and do our staff feel well supported? "People first" is a great slogan, but combining it with our company environment of relaxed productivity meant the working environment became a fun place to be. I think we already mentioned the recent Gallup poll that reported companies with a highly engaged workforce are 21 percent more profitable.[55]

People are not your most important asset. The right people are.

—JIM COLLINS

We stayed one step ahead of our rapid growth by attracting top talent who came from the direction we were headed and fit our mission and values. Many candidates were assessed, but only a select few made the rigorous cut. We remained relentlessly focused on People First, one of Jim Collins's priorities (author of *From Good to Great* and *Built to Last*).

We stayed true to our purpose: providing comprehensive ambulatory and home-based infusion services to both acute and chronically ill patients. As it still says on our website today: "Our compassionate team of experts deliver a cost-effective and seamless care experience that surpasses all others." Patient and employee surveys confirm incredibly high ratings in all areas, year after year.

We communicated. We showed appreciation and stayed focused. We were so obviously responsible and accountable (and we were getting the bottom-line results) that our PE partner let us run the business without interference.

Simple organizational structure and clear accountability
are necessary conditions for the exercise of effective leadership.

—JOHN ADAIR

---

55   White, "8 Employee Engagement Statistics."

We installed internal systems to provide early-warning signals to guard against growing too quickly. Employee engagement and patient satisfaction surveys and quality metrics became our primary KPIs. We delivered on our value proposition, and we exceeded our financial targets. The growth we achieved and sustained would have been impossible without staying true to our shared vision, trust, commitment, and accountability.

Having a vision, mission, and values that we'd all signed on for motivated individuals to step up and even step aside when critical changes needed to be made. When our early radar system forecast bumps in the road ahead, we made tough decisions early. If we needed to pause, we did. Our senior leadership team put the company ahead of any single person.

David, our CEO, kept his hand steady on the wheel as we navigated these big changes, always referencing our purpose and ruthlessly assessing the impact we were having.

And I just kept letting go.

We all let go of the vine.

This *had* to start with me. I actually fired myself, which meant that I quit micromanaging everything and assumed the chairman role. David let go of operational tasks so he could laser focus on what really mattered. Senior leaders felt empowered, so they empowered others.

> **Having a vision, mission, and values that we'd all signed on for motivated individuals to step up.**

Finally, we always celebrated our wins and were deliberate about recognition. It may sound obvious, but it's amazing how often this gets forgotten, especially when an organization grows fasts and success shows up.

The more you praise and celebrate your life,
the more there is in life to celebrate.

—OPRAH WINFREY

Palmetto has become a garden that we manage with tender loving care. As of this writing, we have thirty-nine centers in six states, about five hundred full- and part-time employees, and twelve thousand patients. Our current valuation hovers around $400 million, and we continue to grow at over 35 percent annually.

> *Five million dollars. That's what Medicare offers us at the start of the pandemic. Fantastic! Free money, right? Except, we don't need it. More importantly, we make all of our decisions in accordance with our mission, vision, and values. One of those values is to always do the right thing.*
>
> *We return the money. A year later we get a look at the paperwork Medicare is sending out. Turns out that free money wasn't so free!*

YOUR TURN

Here's our top eighteen recommendations for putting the SPL into action in your organization. Visit successparadoxbook.com to download this checklist for a company scorecard.

1. Housecleaning before growth.

   Who's doing what in your company and why? Is everyone in the right seat on your bus, and who's driving? Dare to challenge the prevailing norm, even about yourself. You may be the problem (like I was).

2. Incentivize growth.

   How will you measure success and what rewards will you offer? Transparency is vital, so everyone knows who gets what and why. Some will be motivated, some won't.

3. Develop your multiyear strategic plan.

   You may know how to create a strategic plan. If not, hire help. Napoleon Hill said that a dream is a goal with a deadline. Be specific.

4. Formulate your vision, mission, and values.

   Your vision describes what you intend to achieve and become in the future. A mission statement communicates your organization's purpose. Values detail your core principles and ethics.

5. Develop your senior leadership team.

   Consider skills, communication styles, diversity, and chemistry. Once you have your team set, step back and ask, "Who's missing?" You might be surprised. Think diversity. Ensure that everyone knows the team is a work in progress; it will evolve.

6. Create a succession plan for all senior leaders.

   Only one-third of organizations have succession plans. Three-quarters of all new senior leaders are not prepared for their jobs. Only one-quarter of all organizations offer the resources necessary to support elevation into C-level roles. Be prepared.[56]

---

56   Ryan Daly, "21 Shocking Statistics on the State of Succession Planning," Aiir Consulting, August 24, 2020, https://aiirconsulting.com/resource/21-shocking-statistics-on-the-state-of-succession-planning/.

7. Transparency.

   When everyone knows what they need to know and feels encouraged to expose what's important without fear of retribution, innovation flourishes.

8. Communication.

   Refine your interview process with professional guidance. Become unrelentingly professional with regular meetings so that everyone knows what to expect. Add spontaneity and fun so that meetings are enjoyable. Demand respectful communication from everyone, regardless of position in your hierarchy.

9. Graduate from isolated silos to collaborating teams.

   Be deliberate and persistent in encouraging active collaboration between individuals and departments, without inadvertently creating unnecessary bureaucracy. Shared goals can be helpful. Incentivize teamwork.

10. Use scorecards that everyone sees.

   We use the EOS scorecard system from the *Traction* book by Gino Wickman and recommend it, but do your own research to determine the best one for you. Regular measurement is a necessity, not an option.

11. Improve your employee orientation process.

   Train new hires with the "be, do, share" principles. Learn if and how candidates might fit into your teams. Communicate clearly about the culture they will be contributing to.

12. Hire to stay ahead of the curve.

    Employee well-being and customer satisfaction are more important than hitting the numbers. Listen when you hear about overwork, mounting stress levels, and missed deadlines. Keep the culture healthy.

13. Maintain a relentless focus on people first.

    Money comes and goes; you want to retain talent. Develop a family feeling in your organization. Make sure everyone feels welcome to share personal concerns that may be affecting their performance. Big company small.

14. Develop realistic performance standards.

    Make sure that everyone understands what constitutes success in your organization and uses the same measurement system. Hierarchy should never suppress honesty.

15. Focus on purpose by staying true to your vision, mission, and values.

    These need to be clearly, succinctly articulated and visited regularly by everyone. Develop protocols for keeping vision, mission, and values vividly alive in daily operations.

16. Be responsible, successful, and accountable enough that PE partners don't feel the need to interfere.

    Investors want assurances that your company is being responsibly managed. Stay ahead of the curve on communication, giving them what they need before they ask for it. Be honest about problems and the solutions you are developing. Address any rumors they may have heard; take them seriously.

17. Let go of the vine.

    Inviting a higher power into the boardroom opens the way for paradoxical success. Be patient. Over time, you'll get used to being somewhat mystified but always grateful for how your organization begins to thrive, without your heroic interventions.

18. Celebrate your wins and give recognition.

    It's easy to forget this when we're growing fast. Acknowledgement is a powerful incentive; use it.

Do what you can in your organization. Reach out to us for help when you need it. If you doubt that this stuff could work in your organization, remember: you'll see it when you believe it!

Surrender and win.

The Means Determine the End

The end justifies the means, right?

That traditional approach invites conflict between personal and organizational values.

In fact, whatever we do along the way will always show up in our end product.

Chefs know this.
Salt tastes different than sugar;
every ingredient influences taste.
Embrace the Lifestyle.

Stay true to your vision, mission, and values.
Live the "be, do, share" principles.

Your results will dependably reflect your process.

CHAPTER THIRTEEN

Surrender and Win

A goal without real consequences is wishful thinking.
Good follow-through doesn't depend on the right
intentions. It depends on the right incentives.

—TIM FERRISS

THIS IS OUR FINAL CHAPTER. Statistically, less than half of all readers actually finish reading a book. And for every thousand aspiring writers who start, fewer than thirty ever finish writing their book. So, congrats to us all for getting here. What now?

The sole purpose of knowledge is to create hunger for experience.

—TEMITOPE IBRAHIM

Our final paradox reminds me of a joke about the means justifying the end. There are a ton of heavy examples, but I like this funny one:

A father in Seattle calls his son in Chicago to announce that he
and his mother are divorcing. "What?" the son exclaims. "You
can't do that, not after forty years of marriage!"

The son calls his sister in Sydney, Australia. She's horrified and immediately calls home, telling their parents that she and her brother are flying there immediately.

Back in Seattle the father chuckles and tells his wife: "That did it. They're both coming home for Thanksgiving, and they're paying for their own plane tickets!"

THE HERO'S JOURNEY

We've referenced the hero's journey a few times. Here we are nearing the end of the third act. Traditionally, the hero leaves their familiar world, travels through an underworld where they learn and suffer and heal and transform, to finally emerge, bringing an "elixir" (something of great value), back with them.

"The hero returns to reality, or the ordinary world, with a prize or understanding. For example, the elixir can be an object or something the hero learned. The hero must bring something back or will end up repeating the journey. The elixir brings closure to the hero. The elixir or treasure helps the hero move on with life."[57]

I completed my journey (for now) and brought back what I learned, which I've shared with you in this book. This brings closure for me and hopefully offers value to you and others, proven strategies for achieving success without damaging bodies and relationships through addictive behaviors and obsessive overwork (like I did).

I was motivated to write this book by the suicide of one of my kids' young friends. Working in the health care field, I'm accustomed to illness and death, but Jack's suicide, this young man with a full life ahead

---

57 "The Return with the Elixir," A Hero's Journey, accessed September 4, 2022, https://projectherosjourney.weebly.com/the-return-with-the-elixir.html.

of him, that was heartbreaking—so sad, devastating, confusing, leaving his family and friends with questions that may go unanswered forever.

CONFRONTING AN EPIDEMIC

We need to acknowledge and confront the serious and escalating mental health problems tormenting so many teenagers and adults today. My personal experience of this, and my daughter's, has convinced me that we need much better support systems. This will require leadership, which is why we wrote this book, to pull the curtain back on the dark side of "success," and provide a game plan for those who feel called to explore this alternative, prove that it works in their lives, and then reach out to help others, especially those challenged by mental health issues like I was.

> We need to acknowledge and confront the serious and escalating mental health problems tormenting so many teenagers and adults today.

> *Mental health ... is not a destination, but a process.*
> *It's about how you drive, not where you're going.*
> **—NOAM SHPANCER, PHD**

This book is just the beginning. My writing partner and I have formed a nonprofit organization, the OpenMind Fitness Foundation (www.openmindfitnessfoundation.org), to fill the gap. While the field of mental health is the domain of professionals, mental wellness is the domain of individuals. But we're not supported to do much for ourselves.

Think about what we do to maintain our physical health. Ideally, we exercise, eat sensibly, and seek out the help we need (seeing our doctor for regular checkups and treating problems as they arise, before they become an emergency). Physical wellness practices are a normal part of our lives. We sure can't say the same for mental health.

We go to the gym for our bodies; where do we go for our minds? Let's be honest about this: mental illness carries a stigma in our society that makes us hesitant to talk about our mental problems, let alone do anything about them. We wouldn't think twice about telling someone that our shoulder was hurting. How about admitting we're depressed or chronically anxious? Oops, that's forbidden territory in "polite" society.

What does the average person do for mental "preventative maintenance?" Next to nothing. We hear that doing crossword puzzles is good for the brain as we age ... that's about it. Prayer, meditation, spending time in nature, learning to rest amid busyness, managing self-talk, and learning how to experience deep emotion in healthy ways ... these are all important for maintaining mental health.

Doctors are grateful when their patients take care of their physical health. Mental health professionals must be just as happy when their patients take preventative measures to maintain their own mental wellness.

Our vision is to help bring mental wellness practices into the mainstream. Our mission is to provide easy and comprehensive access to resources for mental wellness self-care. Our values include gratitude, appreciation, compassion, empathy, and generosity.

SHARING THE WEALTH

Remember Harriet Tubman? We wrote about how she was compelled to go back to free other slaves, rather than just enjoy her own freedom. If what you've experienced reading this book is helping make your life better, please follow her example. Make it about others too, not just yourself.

Start by reaching out to let us know if you want to help. It may be as simple as learning how to talk with your own kids or with other parents, or you might feel called to a more significant role. You can't give what you don't have, so whatever you want to offer others must start with you improving your own mental well-being.

We've offered a series of exercises and practices for this throughout the book. We've produced short audio programs for those who prefer to listen. And we've created a study guide that can be used by churches and businesses and community groups. It includes discussion materials, based on our thirteen paradoxes, recommended formats for meetings, and guidance for facilitators. There's no charge for these materials, the book is available at a discount for study groups, and we are making ourselves personally available to help in any way we can.

For starters, we are interested in your stories. What happens as you shed your own version of dinosaur thinking around success? Perhaps you'd like to jump on a podcast with us to share your insights? We're laying the foundations for a mental wellness support community; you may want to help build it.

We're also planning other books, aimed at specific populations, starting with teenagers at risk, single parents, working women, minority groups, elders struggling with end-of-life issues, etc. We'll need coauthors. Again, that might be you.

If you are interested in finding out more, contact us at www.openmindfitnessfoundation.org.

You cannot begin, until you begin.

—TONY CLEAVER

THE POWER OF FEELING

Remember how we incentivized our Palmetto team, with cash bonuses for hitting the numbers? News flash: the real incentive was something else. Yes, the money mattered, absolutely. But everyone busted their butts because of a feeling. Vision, mission, values ... every single team member knew (and knows now) that success to us means more than financial profit. We are motivated to help more patients in better ways and reduce suffering.

The most effective incentives are feeling-based.

We *have* to feel something for incentives to work. I felt despair about how I'd destroyed my body and my life. I felt remorse for the people I hurt along the way. I felt overwhelming grief when I learned about Jack's suicide. I felt numbing embarrassment when I confronted how I'd hurt my family. And then I felt hope when I surrendered my willpower to let God work through me, rather than trying to be God myself.

If you plan to build a tall house of virtues,
you must first lay deep foundations of humility.

—AUGUSTINE

So, what do *you* feel? Having read the book, having learned how I turned my life and businesses around, having studied what we're recommending to transform your own life and business, what could motivate you to follow through? I'll give you a few minutes to let all this simmer while I tell two stories, one about a neighbor here on Pawleys Island in South Carolina and one about myself.

Charlie is an astronaut, one of only sixteen men who's walked on the moon. He was also an atheist who realized that, despite this grand achievement, he had many regrets about his failures as a husband and a father. He weeps when he recalls the moment he stood on the moon looking down at the earth and felt … well, as he tells it, the miracle he witnessed confirmed that there *had* to be a God.

What he felt changed him for the rest of his life.

My moment started on a beach after three days of desperate soul searching. David and I had just returned from an event in Florida, and the Covid quarantine went into effect the next day. We strategized in our conference room, and I can still recall the scene.

I'm pointing at the screen where we're studying graphs and numbers to figure out how to adjust our communication portals and systems to handle everything remotely, to answer questions, to manage patients, etc. I'm talking. A lot. And something's not right. I notice David, our new CEO, staring at me, and I hear his silent question: "Who's in charge here?"

I flee the room. I find another office to operate from and fire off an email to our CFO, letting her know what the rent will be. She tells me that she'll need David's approval for this. Hell flies into me. I'm furious. I wait. And I wait. Days go by. Finally, I've had enough. I write an email complaining about being left out of decision-making and I rewrite it four times. Before I hit Send, I email Sharon, our coach. She phones me immediately.

"Gary," she barks, "you're being a coward. You worked so hard for the last two years to earn your reputation back and build

your company on trust. Now you're about to destroy it all. I hope you haven't sent that email, but if you have, you deserve whatever you get."

I erase the email and hit the beach instead of Send. I'm grief stricken, feeling lost and worthless. I hear a panicked voice in my head: "I need to feel needed! This is my identity!" I become frantic. "I'm not the CEO anymore, just the chairman, and I don't know what to do or how I fit in."

A mental haze settles over me, and suddenly my own "standing on the moon" moment comes. I let go. I stop trying to figure it out. I ask God. I remember what happened when I did that before, and this experience is just as vivid. Relaxation pours through me. I know one thing. I know that it's all going to work out.

I consult my "compass," the one that Coach Sharon helped me create: mission statement, vision statement, values, plus my one-, three-, and five-year goals all clearly outlined. Well reminded of my priorities, I avoid self-pity. Instead, I'm filled with gratitude, recharged. Without that compass ... well, it doesn't take long to drift away from what's most important when you don't have guidance. And patience.

A highly developed values system is like a compass. It serves as a guide to point you in the right direction when you are lost.

—IDOWU KOYENIKAN

I left that beach and waited ... patiently. David and Sharon redefined roles within the organization, including mine. Without my input. I eventually began working from that new office and settled into appropriate contributions. Everything changed, and it was nothing short of miraculous. I was at peace, in myself and in the organization. That feeling of relaxed productivity has never left me. And I'm prospering as founder and chairman of a private equity sponsored company.

What is now proved was once only imagined.

—WILLIAM BLAKE

So, what about you? I wonder if we could set up a moment for you right now, to create a feeling to center whatever incentives you create for yourself? Let's give it a shot.

SURRENDER AND WIN ... RIGHT NOW!

Find a private spot where you won't be disturbed for ten or fifteen minutes and settle into a comfortable chair. Bring a pen and writing pad. Follow these instructions and do the exercise at your own speed.

Pick a moment one year in the future, today's date. You're going to celebrate your success, imagining that it's already happened.

Think about what success will look like for you,
personally and in your business.

Start with your business. Use a separate piece of paper or your journal for this, landscape style (side way long) and hang onto it. We recommend you consult this regularly and revise it as you go along.

You'll be filling out three columns. On the left, list what you'd like to achieve under the heading: GOALS. Title the middle column WHY and write beside each item. Record your reasons for wanting to achieve those goals. Let's say you have a goal to grow revenue in your company by 10 percent. Why? Becoming more profitable is actually a result. The goal might be to help more people. And the why could be because there's a specific lack in the field you're working in, and you feel called to fill it. Or, like me, because your heart broke, and you're determined to remedy some social failing.

Title the right-side column INCENTIVES. What's in it for you? Think of the personal rewards you'd like to gain from achieving each goal, and don't be shy. Record both the thing and the feeling. For instance: "Trip to Maui, to feel renewed." Now make another list for your personal life and do the same.

GOALS	WHY?	INCENTIVES

Servant leaders deserve what they earn.

Of course, even the best plans get sidetracked. That's OK. Planes are off course most of the time, yet they reach their destinations by constant course correcting. We do the same … when we have a proper compass, a map, and when our minds are guided by a higher intelligence. This takes us right back to where we started in the introduction: surrender and win. Let go to a higher power. That's where the guidance comes from.

All I have seen teaches me to trust the creator for all I have not seen.
—RALPH WALDO EMERSON

THE LAST PARADOX

According to an urban myth, decades old now, a bright young man once marched into a toothpaste company and announced that he knew how they could increase their profits significantly. Dubious but intrigued, the CEO agreed to pay him *if* he could deliver on his promise.

The confident young man agreed and produced his solution: "Make the hole bigger!" They enlarged the toothpaste hole from 5 to 6 mm, and their profits increased by 40 percent.[58]

Making the hole bigger meant customers used more toothpaste, so they bought more often. But they were wasting toothpaste. The result was profit for the company but a loss of resources in the world at large. They were obeying the traditional model: the end justifies the means. Their "end" was profit. Their "means" was to waste resources.

---

58   Sanjiban Roy, "Myth or Fact: The Story of a Renowned Toothpaste Company," Open Web Solutions, January 16, 2017, https://openwebsolutions.in/blog/myth-fact-story-renowned-toothpaste-company/.

If they had been honoring our last paradox—the means determine the end—they would have made the hole smaller, or left it the same. Would this have somehow resulted in more profit? They never gave themselves the chance to find out. But traditional profit-motivated practices *have* made our global environment toxic.

> *When profit is unshared, it's less likely to grow greater.*
> **—MALCOLM FORBES**

When we embrace this paradox, there's no compromise and no harmful side effects. Our "means" prioritize doing good over doing well. This always shows up in the "end." A big company will feel like a small company. But developing that kind of corporate environment, where relaxed productivity is the norm, has to start at the top. That might be you.

> *Profit is a reflection of our vision, mission, and values.*

Remember that partner I helped who tipped me off to buying Palmetto, the one who returned the favor a thousand-fold? This book wouldn't be in your hands right now without her (and she's going to get one of the first signed copies!). This proves the ultimate business paradox:

> *Stop trying to make a profit ... and make a profit!*

SURRENDER

Get ready for a peak experience of what we're talking about. If possible, access the audio program on the website, successparadoxbook.com. You can also read these instructions through, then close your eyes for the experience. You can repeat this whenever you wish. When reading, this marker [...] indicates a pause for contemplation.

Settling into a private, quiet place where you won't be disturbed, phone off, sitting comfortably, begin daydreaming about your life and your business. No structure, no agenda, just let your thoughts flow. What would an ideal future look like? Make your imagined scenario as detailed as possible, involving all your senses.

It's important to close your eyes for this, to create a deep feeling experience. So if you're reading rather than listening, finish these instructions, then close your eyes and follow along from memory.

1. Daydream with a sense of curiosity. What if? Imagine that future success for both your life and your business. Tune in to the feeling of what that would be like. ...

2. Connect with a higher power (whatever that means to you). Silently say to yourself: "Please, help me." You may do this in a prayerful way, imagining you are talking with God. You may just fling the question into a formless void and then listen for what echoes back. ...

3. "Thank you." Say it silently, focusing a feeling of gratitude for receiving the help you need. Repeat it like a mantra, experiencing that emotion in a deep way. ...

4. Let go. You are no longer in control of your life. You have surrendered. Feel the relief that comes with that, knowing that your future is in good hands. Sit in this glow as long as you wish.

Get ready to win.

THE END IS A BEGINNING

You'll need to trust the process to experience the effectiveness of the Success Paradox for yourself. It *can* become your operating system, but you'll need support to install this upgrade and memorize the new internal commands. Visit successparadoxbook.com to connect with fellow travelers exploring this path.

The Success Paradox follows a simple formula: be, do, share. It's new. In fact, it came into focus as we wrote the book. What's next are the field trials. We're hoping that some of you will feel motivated to dig deep into this material, begin living the Lifestyle, develop your own personal turnaround, then reach out to help others. That's the way the formula works.

Being inspires doing inspires sharing.

The Success Paradox follows a simple formula: be, do, share.

Enjoy experimenting with what you've learned, be surprised with the wonderful things you discover about yourself and your organization, and stay in touch.

We shall not cease from exploration,
and the end of all our exploring will be to arrive where we started
and know the place for the first time.

—T.S. ELIOT

Success, happiness, health, loving relationships, and a meaningful life are all dependent on mental well-being.

Despite this undeniable fact, mental health remains a taboo subject in polite culture, hence the global epidemic of mental illness.

We have formed a foundation to educate and innovate in the mental health field, with the objective of making initiatives that support mental fitness as accepted in mainstream society as physical fitness programs have become.

Our first offering, and a gift for readers, is NEXT, a 13-question quiz to determine how mind state determines our ability to make positive life changes, with personalized analysis and recommendations.

It's available free of charge at www.NextTest.org.

www.OpenMindFitnessFoundation.org

BEGIN learning and mastering the Success Paradox Lifestyle

Are you being your authentic self? Do you understand the value of helping others as a business priority? Are you experiencing financial abundance?

➜ Access the Success Paradox Lifestyle Check In to establish your starting point on this learning adventure through the QR code below.

CIRCLE UP with the Success Paradox Lifestyle Study Guide

Download this companion to the book, complete with curriculum and facilitator guidance for creating small discussion groups in homes and churches.

➜ Download the study guide through the QR code below.

LISTEN to audio programs for guidance through experiential exercises

Some of us learn better by listening than reading. Explore the inventory of studio-produced audio programs to accompany and enhance the written guidance in the book.

→ Listen through the QR code below.

JOIN the Success Paradox community online.

Enjoy our online discussion forum. Connect with others who are learning and living the Lifestyle. Find out about coaching and training programs, live and recorded, online and in person.

→ Register through the QR code below to receive regular updates.

Visit us online at www.successparadoxbook.com to access these free resources:

GLOSSARY OF UNIQUE TERMS

A BIG COMPANY THAT FEELS SMALL   Maintaining the mom-and-pop experience for staff and customers, as you grow larger.

BE, DO, SHARE   The three principles of the Success Paradox Lifestyle (SPL): Be authentic, do good, do well.

BEING AUTHENTIC   Being your true self as an everyday priority.

BUSYNESSES   Organizations that are overly, inefficiently busy.

CHASING   Pursuing success and happiness from the outside.

DO-AHOLIC   Someone addicted to doing.

DOING GOOD   Contributing positively to the lives of others.

DOING THE OPPOSITE   Paradoxical thinking that leads to a changed mindset and novel behaviors.

DOING WELL   Being financially prosperous.

FATHER-SON RELATIONSHIP Resolved by giving our lives over to a higher power.

FULL-PROFIT An economic alternative to for-profit and nonprofit businesses, where abundance is shared.

FUTURE THINKING The ability to conceive of the future and take steps now to improve it.

GIVING UP Trading willpower for willingness to let universal wisdom direct our lives.

GOD One name for the intelligent, loving presence that created all life and sustains us.

HEART COMPASS Being guided by the feeling of an envisioned future result.

HIGHER POWER God, universal wisdom, life force ... there are many names for what sustains life.

HO'OPONOPONO An ancient Hawaiian forgiveness ritual.

LETTING VS. MAKING THINGS HAPPEN Paradoxical success depends on letting go, which means we learn to stop pushing to get results.

MENTAL WELLNESS An emerging field of self-care for mental health.

NO IS A COMPLETE SENTENCE The most successful people say no to most things so they can focus on their yes.

PAUSE BUTTON Sometimes we need to pause amid our busyness for a moment of rest to reboot our experience.

PEAK EXPERIENCES Epiphanies may be random or earned, making us feel powerful and helpless.

PRECESSION A Buckminster Fuller term that describes the accumulating value of positive "side effects" as we progress toward our goals.

PREVENTATIVE MAINTENANCE Being consciously alert to course correct as needed can save a life and a business.

RELAXED PRODUCTIVITY The ideal state where being leads to doing and effortless efficiency creates optimum results.

SAY WHAT YOU MEAN WITHOUT SAYING IT MEAN We all dislike conflict, but we can learn how to communicate hard truths with kindness.

SELF-SUFFICIENCY A modern myth that has separated big achievers from the help they need.

SIGNATURE Our personal energetic presence is as unique as our signature.

SPL Success Paradox Lifestyle.

STRUCTURAL TENSION A term coined by author Robert Fritz to describe the relationship between our current reality and an envisioned future.

SURRENDERING CONTROL TO A HIGHER POWER	The first and most important step for learning and living the Success Paradox Lifestyle (SPL).
THE BLESSING OF GRIEF	When we connect our suffering with the suffering of others, we transcend separation and experience the joy within sadness.
THE DRAMA TRIANGLE	A description of dysfunctional relationships between victim, persecutor, and rescuer.
THE HERO'S JOURNEY	The classic storytelling structure in three acts.
THE IMPOSTER SYNDROME	Fear that you will be discovered as incompetent.
THE SUCCESS PARADOX LIFESTYLE (SPL)	Surrendering and winning in life and business, every day.
TOUGH LOVE	What a friend gives us when we most need to hear the truth.
TURNING POINT	The moment in a life or a business when a dramatically new direction is taken.

PRAYER IS
TALKING
TO GOD.

MEDITATION IS
LISTENING
TO GOD.